SUPER FUN
FOR ONE

SUPER FUN FOR ONE

366 Solo Activities for Kids

PATRICIA GORDON
AND
REED C. SNOW

ANDREWS AND McMEEL
A Universal Press Syndicate Company
Kansas City

Library of Congress Cataloging-in-Publication Data

Gordon, Patricia, 1938–
   Super fun for one : 366 solo activities for kids / by Patricia Gordon and Reed C. Snow.
     p.   cm.
   ISBN 0-8362-2161-3 (pbk.)
   1. Games for one. 2. Creative activities and seat work.
I. Snow, Reed C., 1934– . II. Title.
GV1201.39.G67 1996
793'.01922—dc20   96–15943
                                CIP

CONTENTS

FIVE-MINUTE ACTIVITIES

FIFTEEN-MINUTE ACTIVITIES

THIRTY-MINUTE ACTIVITIES

CONTENTS

SIXTY-MINUTE ACTIVITIES

CONTENTS

ACKNOWLEDGMENTS

Thank you, Loretta Gaunt, day-care director extraordinaire at St. Albans Country Day School, Roseville, Calif., for sharing your years of experience in creative play with children, and to LaNae Snow for your encouraging support and assistance.

INTRODUCTION

This is a book for kids and parents. It's for all the kids who need something to do when there's no one to play with. It's also for the busy moms and dads who need something for their *kids* to do when the grown-ups need a break.

What child wouldn't want to try walking barefoot around a room with a penny on top of each big toe? What a challenge! Or how about creating a sculpture out of frozen peas? Think of the many times when kids need a timeout from doing homework, or when they're waiting impatiently to join their playmates and there's nothing to do.

Parents need their own time, too! What parent doesn't need time to unwind from a stressful day, make a business call, or finish making dinner? Parents, here's the help you've been looking for! The activities in the book are not intended to replace valued family together time, but to allow for some individual quality time for you and your children.

Go ahead and browse through these 366 fun activities, some tried and true, some crazy and new—all of which will keep kids happily occupied all by themselves. Is this possible? Yes! We feel that children really can and should be given the opportunity to play all alone and do something creative and fun that will lead to a sense of accomplishment.

The hands-on indoor and outdoor adventures in the book are organized in segments of **Five Minutes, Fifteen Minutes, Thirty Minutes,** and **Sixty Minutes. The plan** gives a simple description of every solo activity, and **What it takes** tells the child exactly what materials are needed. The activities require minimal preparation time, and the instructions are kid-friendly.

After many years of teaching and working with children of all ages, including our own, we have seen the benefits of helping children learn to work and play independently. Self-confidence and self-image are increased; creativity and problem-solving skills are developed. What could be more rewarding than seeing an expression of satisfaction and hearing your child proudly exclaim, "I did it all by myself"?

The activities in this book have been gathered and collected over many years from colleagues in the teaching profession, from day-care and scout directors, from church and camp leaders, and from ideas shared with us by our own children. We hope that your children will have as much fun doing the activities as we have had collecting and creating them.

PATRICIA GORDON
REED C. SNOW

FIVE-MINUTE ACTIVITIES

Why sit and look out the window or watch another boring TV commercial when you could spend that time doing something really crazy like creating a picture by tearing up a piece of paper behind your back? That's right! Try this and all of the other **Five-Minute Activities** guaranteed to perk up those tiny dull moments when there's no one to play with.

1. BEHIND YOUR BACK

 The plan: You're going to actually create a picture by "tearing it up" behind your back!

What it takes:
• Several pieces of paper (used, if possible)

Are you ready to "tear up" a piece of paper into a masterpiece? Get ready, because this is quite a challenge. While standing up, hold a piece of paper with both hands behind your back. Now, decide what you want to make, but be sure it's something simple. You're going to create this work of art by tearing it out of the paper, as you continue to hold it behind your back. Making (tearing) a basketball might sound easy, but go on, give it a try. It's not as simple as you think! When you've finished, take a look at your masterpiece!

When you get the feel of it you can try making something a little more complicated like a bird. Take your time. Make those little tears carefully. You're going to be amazed at how challenging this really is. Ideas: a car, Halloween cat, tree, airplane, maybe even a self-portrait!

2. PROMISES, PROMISES!

 The plan: Make coupons or tickets that you can give to friends or family members!

What it takes:
• Ruler
• Pencil
• Any size drawing or colored paper, old stationery, or note cards
• Colored marking pens or crayons
• Scissors

Use a ruler and your pencil to draw a large square or rectangle on the paper. This is going to be your coupon or ticket, and any fun shape will really do. You may even want to try making up a coupon shape of your own. Something shaped like a drop of water or even an airplane would be unusual and interesting.

Now all you have to do is write a "promise" on your coupon of something you will do for someone else. Let's see . . . maybe a coupon for walking the dog or folding the towels when they come out of the dryer would be a great promise. A coupon for reading a story to a younger brother, sister, or friend would really be appreciated.

You can decorate your coupon and cut it out with scissors. Now you're ready to give your coupon to a special someone. Wouldn't it be a wonderful surprise if you gave your teacher a coupon that would be good for tidying up your classroom?

3. SOCK IT TO 'EM

The plan: Become a basketball star in your own living room!
What it takes:
- 2–5 pairs of socks
- Empty wastebasket, bucket, or large pan
- Watch or clock that displays seconds

Before you begin this game, make sure the room is clear of any breakable objects. Now roll a few pairs of socks together to make separate balls. Place the empty wastebasket, bucket, or pan against a wall and shoot your "ball" into the "basket." There's no slam-dunking in this game, but consider any or all of these Sock It to 'Em challenges:

#1: Start shooting from five steps away and see how many baskets you can make in a row without missing. When you're really good at shooting from one distance, move back a few steps and start counting your baskets from there. You'll be amazed at how quickly you improve.

#2: Try making different types of shots, like underhanded, hook, left-handed only, right-handed only, jump, or any other creative shots you can think of. How about your-back-to-the-basket-over-the-head shot, or a sitting-on-the-floor-looking-at-the-ceiling shot? You can also try a "football hike" shot between your legs, with your back facing the "basket."

#3: Have your own MBA three-point shootout. Use a watch or clock that displays seconds to see how many baskets you can make in three minutes or more from three different locations.

4. QUARTER SPIN

 The plan: See how long you can keep a quarter (or another coin) spinning on its side!

What it takes:
- 1 quarter, nickel, dime, or penny
- Table with a smooth surface
- Watch or clock that displays seconds

Hold a quarter or other coin between your thumb and first two fingers. Stand the quarter on its edge on the table, twisting your hand and wrist to make the quarter spin. Let go of the quarter and see how long it keeps moving. Can you get it to stay on its side?

Time your spinning coin with a watch or clock and see how many seconds you can keep the quarter spinning. Don't worry if you don't have a watch. All you have to do is count out loud, starting with the number "1." Can you keep the quarter spinning up to the count of 10? Try spinning and timing other coins, and find out which coin spins the longest.

5. LOVE NOTES

 The plan: Surprise people you care about with little decorated "love notes"!

What it takes:
- Plain or colored paper (any type)
- Pencil or pen
- Colored marking pens or crayons

You don't have to be Cupid and it doesn't have to be Valentine's Day to tell someone that you love them or that they're a very special person. All you have to do is fold a piece of paper in half and write a short little "love note" on the front or on the inside. Make up your own message, or maybe all you need to say is "I LOVE YOU." Now dress up your note by drawing and coloring some very loving decorations. Colorful hearts and flowers, birds and butterflies, stars and moons, or boats and planes will bring a happy smile to anyone who is lucky enough to receive one of your notes. The fun part is deciding where to place your note. On top of Mom's pillow? On the driver's seat in Dad's car? On a shelf in the refrigerator? Maybe even in your brother's bookbag.

6. FOILED AGAIN

 The plan: Create wonderful aluminum foil sculptures!
What it takes:
- 5 or 6 small rocks
- Small box (like the size costume jewelry may be in)
- Box of aluminum foil

In Los Angeles, California, there's a restaurant where waiters make aluminum foil sculpture figures to decorate the boxes for left-over food. It's wacky fun! You can do it, too. Start by putting five or six rocks into the small box to keep it steady. Decide what special sculpture you would like. A snake ready to strike would be great.

Pull off a long piece of foil. Place the small box in the middle of the long foil. Carefully cover the box by pulling the two short sides of foil over the box, leaving the two long ends free.

Bring the two long ends together, right over the top of the box. *Gently* crush the two long pieces of foil together until it looks like a snake rising off the box. Do this very carefully or your snake will get too skinny and tight. Make a snake head on the very top by crushing the tip of the foil into a triangle shape and tilting it toward you. That ought to scare your friends and family!

You might try making a rabbit with two long ears for your next foil sculpture. Rabbits are a lot harder than snakes, but with a little practice, you can do it.

7. BOUNCER

 The plan: See how good you are at *bouncing* a ball into a container.

What it takes:
- 6 plastic containers of different sizes and shapes
- Small rubber ball

This is harder than you think! Begin by placing the containers close together on a hard floor (not carpet) so they are all touching each other. Move back a few steps, and throw the ball *at the floor*, trying to bounce it into one of the containers. See how many bounces it takes in a row before you score a hit. You may even want to set a limit of twenty bounces and count how many times you get the ball into a container. Try breaking your own record!

8. PENNY TOSS

 The plan: Find out how good you are at making "cents" fall into the right containers!

What it takes:
- 6 drinking glasses or jars of different sizes and shapes
- 20 pennies or other coins

Arrange the glasses or jars on the floor by placing them one shoe length apart. You can line them up in a row, or you can place them in a circle or a triangle. Now take two giant steps back from the containers, and see how many pennies you can toss into the jars or glasses. Take a few practice shots to see which method works best, but it's likely that a very gentle underhand toss will work better than an overhand shot. Give each method a try, then toss the pennies one at a time, using your preferred shot.

Now you're ready to test your skill, and see how many of the twenty pennies you can toss into the containers. If you're terrific at subtraction you won't have to count both the pennies in the jars and the ones on the floor. All you'll have to do is pick the pennies up off the floor that "missed the mark" and subtract that number from twenty. Now you'll know how many are in the jars without counting them. Are you a super shot? Are you a super "subtracter"?

9. ICE CREAM, YOUR DREAM

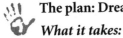 **The plan: Dream up new names for ice cream!**

What it takes:
- Piece of paper
- Pencil

Ice cream! Yum, Yum! Pretend you just became the owner of an ice-cream store, and you have to name all the flavors. Close your eyes and dream of delicious flavors and creamy colors. As you think, use a pencil and a piece of paper to write the vivid names that come into your mind. "Chinese Chocolate" might be a good name for chocolate ice cream with rice crispies. "Elegant Elephant" could be a name for licorice flavor. You can do better than that for sure! When you get the flavor list finished you might dream up a name for your new dream store. "31 Flavors" has already been taken, but you'll come up with a better name. How about "Cones R Us?" Be sure to write it on the paper so you'll be ready to add a new flavor or the name of your store whenever you start to dream.

10. MUFFIN TOSS

 The plan: Toss marbles, rocks, pennies, and paper clips into muffin tin cups!

What it takes:
- 1 muffin tin
- 5 each of marbles, rocks, pennies, and paper clips
- Piece of paper
- Pencil

Place the muffin tin on the floor. Put five marbles, rocks, pennies, and paper clips in your pocket. Walk about two paces away from the muffin tin. Try your luck at tossing the marbles, rocks, pennies, and paper clips into the muffin tin cups. See if you can toss one item into each cup of the muffin tin. Record your successes with the paper and pencil. Be sure to write how many tries it takes to fill the whole tin.

Which items fall into the muffin cups the easiest: the marbles, rocks, pennies, or paper clips? When you have mastered the short distance, increase the challenge. Move a few paces farther away from the muffin tin and try your luck again.

11. LET'S MAKE CENTS!

 The plan: Use pennies and other coins to create a whole treasury of strange characters!

What it takes:
• Two big handfuls of pennies (other coins, too)
• A flat surface

Can you imagine making zoo animals or spaceships or the solar system out of pennies and other coins? Pretend that you're drawing a picture, but instead of a pencil you're using these round objects to form shapes.

All you have to do is arrange the coins on a flat surface to resemble anything you'd like. Five pennies in a straight line make the back of an elephant. Three more pennies curving off from the straight line looks like a trunk. How could you make the legs and body?

Try a few creations until you get the hang of it. In no time you'll be saving your pennies and other change just so you can make bigger coin pictures. If you're creating coin pictures on the floor, please remind everyone, "No vacuuming while the artist is at work!"

12. BILLY BARKER BAKED BROWN BREAD

 The plan: Make up wacky sentences that all begin with the same letter!

What it takes:
- Piece of Paper
- Pencil
- Eraser

Susie **S**ummers **s**aid **s**omething **s**illy **s**o **s**he **s**at **s**ilently. What about this one: **A**rtie **A**ardvark **a**lways **a**te **a**rtichokes **a**t **a**fternoon **a**ctivities! Get your paper and pencil ready, turn on the brain power, and begin making up your own wacky sentences and write them down. All you have to do is start every word of your sentence with the same letter. It's *that* easy! Try doing three sentences to start with, and then maybe you can even do an entire paragraph! **W**acky **w**riters **w**rite **w**onderfully **w**ell!

13. SQUIRT BALL

 The plan: Squirt Ping-Pong balls off plastic soda bottles!
What it takes:
- 3 large plastic soda bottles
- Water
- 3 Ping-Pong balls
- Household squirt bottle

This activity is definitely an outdoor game. Fill the plastic soda bottles half full with water to keep them from tipping over. Place a Ping-Pong ball on top of the opening of each soda bottle.

Fill the household squirt bottle with water. Use the squirt bottle to spray the Ping-Pong balls off the soda bottles. To test your skill see how far you can stand away from the bottles and still knock off the balls!

14. GLUE PICTURES

 The plan: Squeeze glue onto waxed paper; then paint it to look like anything you'd like!

What it takes:

- White glue
- Waxed paper
- Colored marking pens
  or tempera paint
- Paintbrush
- Black fine-tip marking pen

Squeeze some globs of glue onto a piece of waxed paper. Try not to pile it up too thick because it will take too long to dry. When it's completely dry, use marking pens or tempera paint and a paintbrush to make designs on the glue shapes. You can have fun turning the blobs into crazy characters, animals, and funny faces, and after they dry they'll peel right off the waxed paper!

15. HANDPRINT FAMILY

 The plan: Use your handprint to turn fingers into family members!

What it takes:

- Pencil
- Piece of paper
- Colored marking pens or crayons

Handprint families are lots of fun, especially when you include your dog, cat, parakeet, or hamster. You may even have enough fingers left over to include Grandma and Grandpa, aunts, uncles, or cousins.

With your pencil trace around your hand on a piece of paper. A good way to begin your finger family is to turn the tallest finger that you've traced into the tallest person in your family. Make faces on the top of your fingers. Use your pencil to add hair and features. You can even dress these people up by drawing them some terrific clothes. Will everyone be wearing casual clothes like sweatpants and sweatshirts? Maybe you'd like to dress up the group in astronaut suits? Bathing suits? Make them colorful!

16. SNOWY ICE CREAM

The plan: Make some tasty snow cream after the first snowfall of winter!

What it takes:

- Freshly fallen snow
- Bowl
- Spoon
- Granulated sugar
- Vanilla extract
- Cream or milk
- Cocoa powder or instant chocolate powder

Put on your warm clothes, take a bowl and spoon, go outside, and scoop up a bowlful of clean, new-fallen snow.

Sprinkle some sugar, a few drops of vanilla, and a few drops of cream or milk over the snow. Stir until your snow cream is blended. You don't have to measure carefully, but keep sampling as you go so you'll get just the taste you want. If you're a chocolate lover, you'll want to add a little cocoa powder or instant chocolate powder to the mix.

It melts fast, so grab a spoon and dig in!

17. DIVING MASK MAGIC

The plan: You'll be able to see everything underwater with this milk carton diving mask!

What it takes:

- Scissors
- Empty half-gallon milk carton
- Clear plastic wrap
- Rubber bands or transparent tape

Use your scissors to cut the top and the bottom off the milk carton, or ask a grown-up to do it for you. Make the edges straight where you cut. Next, stretch a piece of plastic wrap over one end of the carton and keep it in place with a rubber band or two. You can also use transparent tape to hold it in place. That's all there is to it.

Next time you're in the bathtub, place some plastic objects

on the bottom of the tub. Now take your diving mask and put the plastic wrap end in the water to see what a great viewer this makes. Think of what you could see if you took this to a lake, stream, or the beach!

18. OVER THE EDGE

 The plan: Blow six cotton balls off the end of a table!
What it takes:
- Table (a long one, if possible)
- 6 cotton balls

Place six cotton balls across one end of a table. Stand behind the cotton balls, and blow all six balls off the opposite end of the table. The cotton balls must remain separate and not in a bunch. You must begin again if any of the cotton balls fall off the table sides instead of the end. Take a deep breath and go for it!

19. REPEAT REPEAT

 The plan: Draw a shape and then repeat it inside and out until the paper is filled up!
What it takes:
- Pencil
- Drawing paper
- Black or other color fine-tip marking pens

Use a pencil to draw a shape or a simple design on the drawing paper, such as a heart or a leaf. Now repeat the shape inside of the first one, drawing your lines close to the ones you've just drawn. Repeat the same lines over and over, inside and outside of the shape or design, until the paper is covered. If you draw a heart, you keep drawing the same heart shape inside the original one and outside of the original one. Experiment with different colors and thin lines and fat lines. Your design doesn't even have to look like anything. A free-form design will also look great!

20. POTATO BOWLING

 The plan: Use potatoes for bowling "balls" and see how close you get to hitting the mark!

What it takes:
- Piece of white paper
- Colored marking pen
- 4 potatoes

Draw a large circle on a piece of paper with a marking pen. Place the paper on the floor, and take two giant steps back from the paper. Now see if you can roll (bowl) the potatoes, one at a time, into the circle. See how close you can get! Take another giant step or two back and see if your aim is as good as it was up close. When you get good with one hand, try switching to the other hand. It will feel awkward at first, but keep practicing, and you may end up being the best two-handed potato bowler on the block!

21. HAWAIIAN ALPHABET CHALLENGE

 The plan: Form words by using the twelve letters of the Hawaiian alphabet!

What it takes:
- Piece of paper
- Pencil

The Hawaiian alphabet has only twelve letters: *a, e, i, o, u, h, k, l, m, n, p,* and *w*. Use your pencil to write these letters across the top of your paper. Now see how many English words you can write using only the Hawaiian alphabet. You can repeat letters like the two o's in the word "look" and two ll's in the word "hello." You're pretty good if you wrote more than twenty words.

22. BOTTLE THE OCEAN

 The plan: Watch waves ripple and break in a bottle that you fill with oil and water!

What it takes:
- Clear bottle with a screw-top lid (clean, plastic soda bottle with the label removed works well)
- Bottle of salad oil
- Water
- Blue food coloring

You'll be able to watch how waves form and break in the ocean, and you won't even have to leave your house. Fill a clear bottle one-third full with salad oil. Next, fill the rest of the bottle all the way to the top with water. Add several drops of blue food coloring until your ocean is just the right color, and then screw on the lid tightly.

Hold the bottle in your hand so that it's on its side. Now, rock it slowly back and forth. Watch how the waves begin to form. You have now created your own little ocean in a bottle without even traveling to the beach!

23. TUBE ROLL

 The plan: Roll Ping-Pong balls down a paper tube into plastic bowls!

What it takes:
- 3 plastic bowls
- Wrapping paper tube or paper towel tube
- 3 Ping-Pong balls
- Piece of paper
- Pencil

Set three plastic bowls on the floor about one foot apart. Hold the paper tube at waist level and point it straight down toward one of the bowls. Roll a Ping-Pong ball through the tube aiming for the first bowl. Score ten points if the ball hits and stays in the bowl.

Again hold the tube at waist level, but this time tilt the tube at an angle toward the second bowl. Roll the ball through the tube, and give yourself twenty points if it hits the bowl and stays in.

The third roll is the hardest of all. Hold the tube at waist level, but this time extend your arm and the tube straight out above the third bowl. The ball has much farther to fall this time. Give yourself thirty points if the Ping-Pong ball stays in the third bowl.

A perfect score is sixty points.

24. THREE BAGS FULL

The plan: Toss Ping-Pong balls into paper bags hanging on a clothesline!

What it takes:
- 3 lunch-size paper bags
- Clothesline or string stretched between two chairs
- Pinch-type clothespins
- 6 Ping-Pong balls

Open the paper bags and hang them on a clothesline or string stretched between two chairs with pinch-type clothespins. Stand away from the clothesline, and toss the Ping-Pong balls into the paper bags, two balls to each bag. When you use a string stretched between two chairs, sit down to toss the balls. The farther away you stand or sit from the bags, the harder it is to get "three bags full."

If you're able to fill your bags with two balls each, you win the title of "three bags full champion."

25. CLOUD CHARMERS

The plan: Draw clouds, and turn them into strange characters by giving them features!

What it takes:
- Pencil
- Large piece of white paper
- Colored marking pens

Draw big white fluffy clouds, skinny long clouds, or little puffy clouds that look like cotton balls on a piece of paper. When your paper is covered with lots of different shapes of clouds, you can then turn them into some remarkable-looking characters. Give your clouds eyes, mouths, and noses, maybe even ears. How about having two clouds looking at each other? Maybe one big cloud is a monster cloud that has big teeth and narrow eyes. Could you show one cloud blowing away the other clouds? Or, you could even make an entire cloud family with Mom, Dad, and lots of little clouds! Use marking pens to go over your pencil drawings so they'll show up better. Is there a cloudy day in your weather forecast?

26. SECRET MESSAGES

 The plan: Use waxed paper to write a secret message and watercolors to read it!

What it takes:
- Waxed paper
- Plain writing paper
- Pencil
- Watercolors or tempera paint
- Paintbrush

Place a piece of waxed paper on top of a piece of plain writing paper. Write a message to someone on the waxed paper with your pencil. Be sure to press down hard on the pencil so the wax will transfer to the plain paper, but not so hard that it will tear the waxed paper.

When you deliver your message, tell the person to take some dark-colored "watery" watercolors or tempera paint diluted with a brush full of water, and brush it over the paper. Everywhere there is wax on the paper, the paint will not stick, and the person will be able to read your message. Write a message to yourself, and see how good you are at making the writing appear!

27. NOSE DROPS

 The plan: Drop paper clips from the point of your nose into a plastic soda bottle!

What it takes:
- Plastic soda bottle
- 20 paper clips

This is great practice for your aiming ability. Set a plastic soda bottle on the floor. Hold one paper clip to the tip of your nose. When you think you are aimed directly over the opening of the bottle, let the paper clip fall. If your aim is good, the clip will plonk into the bottle. Try all twenty paper clips and see how skilled you can become.

28. SUNSHINE PRINTS

 The plan: Put leaves or flowers on dark paper and the sun will do the rest!

What it takes:
- A sunny day
- Leaves, twigs, flowers, petals
- Dark-colored construction paper
- Straight pins

Wait for a sunny day to do this activity. Then, go out in your yard and collect a few leaves or maybe a few petals from a flower. A twig or two and some blades of grass might also be a nice touch. Place your collectibles on a piece of dark-colored construction paper on the ground in a spot that will get lots of sunshine all day long. Use straight pins to poke through the leaves or flowers and the paper, and into the ground to hold them down.

Now it's up to the sun to finish the job. Take a peek every now and then and see how things are coming, but after a few hours, you'll see a print on the paper of the objects on top. If you want to do a super sun print someday, get some light-sensitive paper from a hobby store. It takes only a few minutes for this kind of special paper to make a shadow print.

29. BOOMERANG STICK

 The plan: Make a boomerang with two popsicle sticks!

What it takes:
- 2 popsicle sticks
- White glue
- Thread

Cross two popsicle sticks near the top part of each stick to form a tepee or triangle shape. Glue the sticks together where they cross each other in the triangle shape, and let them dry. When they are dry, wrap thread tightly around the glued area to make sure the sticks will not come apart.

Take the boomerang outside and toss it with a flick of your wrist to make it spin. After a few practice tosses your boomerang should come flying back to you.

30. SHAKE, RATTLE, AND ROLL DOUBLES

 The plan: Roll as many doubles with the dice as you can with the help of a third die!

What it takes:
- 3 dice
- Timer or clock
- Piece of paper
- Pencil

Here's the challenge! Roll two dice and see if the numbers match. If the numbers on both dice match, it's called a double. If they do, good for you! If on the first try they do not match, take out the third die and roll it until it matches one of the two dice. Now you're ready to begin the game.

The purpose of this game is to get as many points as possible in five minutes. If you shake doubles on your first roll of the two dice, you get three points. Record this with your pencil on a piece of paper. If you need to use the third die to get a match, score yourself only one point. Time yourself, and keep score for five minutes.

31. PING-PONG DOMINO

 The plan: Knock down ten dominoes with two Ping-Pong balls!

What it takes:
- Piece of paper
- Pencil
- Table
- 10 dominoes
- 2 Ping-Pong balls

With a pencil, draw this pattern on the paper: one dot on the end of the paper closest to you, two dots in a row above it, then three dots in a row, then four dots in a row. Make the dots and rows about two inches apart so that the group of dots form a triangle. Place the paper in the middle of a flat table.

Stand a domino on end on each dot of the paper pattern. Roll the Ping-Pong balls from the edge of the table toward the dominoes. You may roll the balls from any direction, either toward the front, side, or back of the dominoes. The trick is to make the dominoes knock each other down.

32. HUM ON A COMB

 The plan: Wrap a piece of tissue paper over a comb to make a musical instrument!

What it takes:
- Tissue paper
- Comb

Wrap a piece of tissue paper around the teeth of a comb. Now hum into it. Feel the paper vibrate and tickle your lips as you hum. What a funny feeling and strange sound!

33. HOOP IT UP

 The plan: Make paper plate hoops to toss over bottles, doorknobs, or bedposts!

What it takes:
- 3 paper plates
- Scissors
- 4 soda bottles or cans

Cut the centers out of three paper plates with the scissors. You now have three hoops.

Set four soda bottles or cans on the floor about two feet apart. Toss the hoops at the bottles or cans, and see how many times you ring a target. Hoop It Up can be played over doorknobs and bedposts, too.

34. TWENTY-SIX AND YOU WIN!

 The plan: Write lists of items in categories!

What it takes:
- Piece of lined paper
- Pencil

Think of a category like cars, colors, animals, cereals, flowers, or TV shows. Write the name of one category at the top of a piece of paper. Down the left-hand side of the paper, write the twenty-six letters of the alphabet, one letter on each line. Now list one item next to each letter from A to Z under that category. For instance, if your category is cereals, next to the letter "A" you could write Alpha-Bits. The letter "B" could be Bran Flakes. Got it?

Scoring:

5 or less:	Try a new category!
6–10:	You're on your way!
11–22	You've arrived!
23–26	You qualify to write your own dictionary!

35. PENNY LINEUP

The plan: Collect pennies and arrange them by date!

What it takes:

- Pennies
- Pencil
- Lined paper

Collect a handful of pennies. Family members often have a bunch of pennies they forget to use. Sometimes you can even find pennies under couch cushions! When you've gathered the pennies, look at each penny and notice the date. Find the oldest penny and write its year on the paper with a pencil. Find the next oldest penny and write its year on the paper. Place all the pennies with the same date in one stack. Write the dates as you go. Which stack has the most pennies? What year is the newest penny?

Now that you know all the dates on your pennies, put them in a straight line with the oldest penny first and the newest penny last. Did you find a penny from the year you were born?

36. DO BUTTERFLIES FLY?

The plan: Make a beautiful butterfly with wings that will float in the breeze!

What it takes:

- Colored construction paper or plain white paper
- Colored marking pens or crayons
- Scissors
- White glue
- Popsicle stick

Fold a piece of paper in half, and use your scissors to cut a curving piece or a triangle out of each of the four corners. Keep the paper folded so you'll be cutting through two pieces of paper at a time. Open the paper and use your crayons or markers to decorate the "wings." You may want to experiment on how much paper to cut away for just the right butterfly look. Glue the popsicle stick on the inside of the fold of the opened paper. When the glue is dry you can move the butterfly up and down and see how the wings will "fly."

37. SOFTY THE SNOWMAN

 The plan: Create a snowman with marshmallows!

What it takes:

- Paper plate
- 7 marshmallows
- Toothpicks
- Colored construction paper
- Scissors
- White glue

Put seven marshmallows on the paper plate. Take one marshmallow (the head) and push a toothpick halfway into the center, leaving half of the toothpick showing. Take another marshmallow and push it onto the rest of the first toothpick. Now you have a head and the first half of a body. Get a toothpick and push it into the middle of another marshmallow, leaving half of the toothpick showing. Push that piece of toothpick into the top half of the snowman's body.

Now your snowman needs arms and legs. Push a toothpick right through the top body part so you can see the toothpick poking out of both sides. Put marshmallows on either side. The last two marshmallows are for legs. Put a toothpick in the center of each leg and attach them to the lower body. You'll probably have to slant these toothpicks so the snowman can stand firmly on his legs. Use the scissors to cut out eyes, nose, mouth, buttons, and maybe even a belt out of colored construction paper. Glue them on and give your snowman a name.

38. BOOK ID

 The plan: Make identification stickers for your books!

What it takes:

- Roll of brown paper tape or piece of paper
- Scissors
- Colored marking pens or crayons
- White glue

The initials ID are an abbreviation of the word "identification." Each book you own should have your ID on it. Cut off a piece of brown paper tape or a piece of paper about as wide as your hand.

Write your name in the middle of the tape or paper with a black marking pen. Now decorate around your name with bright-colored marking pens or crayons. When you have a book that needs your ID, just lick the back of your tape or place glue on the paper ID, and paste it somewhere in your book, like on the inside of the front cover.

39. JUST ONE MORE

 The plan: See how many toothpicks can be stacked on the opening of a soda bottle!

What it takes:
- Soda bottle with a narrow neck
- Box of toothpicks (flat ones are best)

Here is a challenging but simple game. Place a soda bottle on a flat surface. One at a time put toothpicks across the narrow opening. See how many toothpicks can be stacked before they collapse. The current record holder must be somewhere near thirty toothpicks. Can you beat that?

40. PING-PONG BOUNCERS

 The plan: Use skinny cans to catch bouncing Ping-Pong balls!
What it takes:
- 2 Ping-Pong balls, small Superballs, small bouncing balls
- Skinny can such as a potato chip can, tennis ball can, or a large frozen juice can

This activity takes a great deal of hand-eye coordination, and it's not as easy as it looks. Bounce a Ping-Pong ball onto a hard floor with one hand. Let it bounce one or two times, and with the other hand holding the can, try to catch the ball in the can! Can you scoop it up? Can you get under it in time before it stops bouncing? Can you switch hands and still catch the ball? Are you daring enough to try TWO balls bouncing at the same time, and try to catch both balls? What about TWO balls and TWO cans? Give it a try!

41. TUBE TUNES

 The plan: Create a musical hummer by putting waxed paper over the end of a paper tube!

What it takes:
- Empty paper towel cylinder
- Waxed paper
- Scissors
- Rubber band

You can easily make a musical instrument with an empty paper towel cylinder. Cut a round piece of waxed paper quite a bit larger than the end of the cylinder. Place the waxed paper circle over one end of the cylinder and secure it with a rubber band.

Hum your favorite tune into the open end of the Cylinder Hummer, and you'll be surprised at the crazy sound!

42. ARE YOU THERE?

 The plan: Make a walkie-talkie from paper cups!
What it takes:
- Two paper cups
- Pencil
- Very long piece of string
- Scissors
- 2 toothpicks

Turn the two paper cups upside down on a flat surface. With a sharp pencil poke a small hole in the center of the bottom of each cup. The hole should just be big enough to put a string through. Decide how long your string should be: five paces, ten paces, twenty paces, or even a hundred. Cut the string to the length you want.

Carefully thread one end of the string through the bottom of one cup. Reach your fingers into the cup and catch the end of the string. Pull the string until you have enough to tie the string around the center of a toothpick. The toothpick will keep the string from slipping back through the hole. Do the same thing to the other cup. Use the other end of your string.

When a friend or family member comes to visit, try out your walkie-talkie by stretching the string tightly between the cups. Whisper, "Are you there?" into one cup and see if you can be heard in the other cup!

43. CARPET BALL

The plan: Roll Ping-Pong balls toward a tennis ball target!

What it takes:
- 1 tennis ball
- Piece of ribbon or string
- 3 Ping-Pong balls
- Piece of paper
- Pencil

Carpet Ball is a game that will improve your rolling skill and aim. Place a tennis ball in a clear space on the carpet. Walk away from the tennis ball about ten steps, and put the ribbon down. Stand behind the ribbon and roll the Ping-Pong balls one at a time toward the tennis ball. Give yourself three points on a piece of paper with a pencil every time a Ping-Pong ball stops two or less inches away from the tennis ball. If this is too easy, move the ribbon back a few more steps.

44. SPONGE KNOCK DOWN

The plan: Try to knock down three sponges with a Nerf ball or wadded paper ball!

What it takes:
- Three dry sponges
- Soft sponge Nerf ball or pieces of paper wadded up to make a ball

Clear off a table and stand three sponges up on end. Stand back about eight long steps, and throw the ball at the sponges. See how many tries it takes to knock all three sponges down. Practice the Sponge Knock Down game, and see if you can knock three sponges down in three tries.

45. HOT/COLD-LEFT/RIGHT

 The plan: Up/down are two, and now it's your turn to name as many opposites as you can!

What it takes:
• Piece of paper
• Pencil

Once you get the hang of this little activity you'll be surprised at how many pairs of opposites you'll be able to think up. All you have to do is write down a word that most likely has an opposite meaning. Next, write the word that means the opposite right next to it.

To get you started, here's a few for you to try: **Happy/? High/? Big/?** How did you do? Did you come up with **Happy/Sad, High/ Low, Big/Little?** If you did, you're on your way to uncovering many more "opposites." Get **Going!** or is it **Coming?**

46. PICK 'EM UP!

 The plan: Try this mini version of pick-up sticks using toothpicks, of all things.

What it takes:
• A handful (about 20) of round toothpicks
• Any flat surface

Hold a handful of toothpicks on a table with all of the ends touching the table and all of the toothpicks standing upright. Now very quickly let go, and pull your hand away. Are the toothpicks in a jumbled mess? Perfect!

You now have the job of taking away one toothpick at a time from the pile, as carefully as you possibly can. Once you have one toothpick you can use it as a helper to flip off other toothpicks. This can get very tricky, but see how many you can remove from the stack before one or more of the other toothpicks moves. As soon as you touch a toothpick and another one moves, the game is over. Pick them up, and start all over again! Do you think you can pick them all up without a single jiggle?

SUPER FUN FOR ONE

47. STACK AND SMACK, SNACK-A-BOBS

 The plan: Create your own snack by threading fruit and food pieces on toothpicks!

What it takes:
- Apple, banana, orange, other fruit
- Cheese, bologna, or cooked meat
- Pickles (if you like them)
- Plate
- Table knife
- Toothpicks
- Paper plate

First wash your hands with soap and water. Assemble all of the nutritious food on the plate. Use the table knife to cut the apple and other fruit you have chosen into one-inch chunks. Cut the cheese, meat, or bologna into one-inch pieces also. Pickles might already be the right size.

Now you're ready to put the food chunks onto the toothpicks. Make six or seven Snack-a-Bobs, put them on a paper plate, and you're ready for a delicious treat. Be sure to clean up before tasting!

48. FIELD GOAL FLIP

 The plan: Play this game by flipping wadded paper over a goalpost!

What it takes:
- 2 pieces of paper
- Yardstick
- Scissors
- String
- 2 chairs

First wad the pieces of paper into tight balls. Next use your yardstick to measure a piece of string about twelve inches long. Then cut the string, and tie it between two chairs at a height of either three, six, nine, or twelve inches above the floor. The string is now your goalpost.

Place a paper wad on the floor about six inches away from the string. Use your fingers striking against your thumb to flip a wad of paper over the goalpost. Did your flip score? Each time your wad of paper goes over the goal give yourself two points!

Here's a hint: the higher the string, the harder the challenge. The farther away you are from the goal, the harder it is to flip a goal, just like in the NFL. With some practice you'll be able to flip the wad right in the middle of the goalpost! Imagine the San Francisco 49ers and the Dallas Cowboys tied in the championship game. You're the field goal kicker! Go for it!

49. ANIMAL CRACKERS

 The plan: Pull letters out of a paper bag and write animal names that start with that letter!

What it takes:
- Twenty-six small pieces of paper
- Pencil
- Paper bag
- Piece of lined paper

Write the letters of the alphabet from A to Z on the small pieces of paper. Better start with "A" so you won't leave any letters out. Place all twenty-six lettered pieces into the paper bag.

Put your hand in the bag and bring out one piece of paper. On the piece of lined paper write the letter you picked from the bag. Now quickly write as many animals as you can think of that start with that letter. Next to the letter of the alphabet, write how many animals you listed. Continue pulling letters from the paper bag until your piece of paper is filled with animal names.

For a real challenge, start all over again, and see if you can beat the number of animals you named on the first pick.

50. A PICTURE OF NATURE

 The plan: Learn to write Haiku poetry faster than you can say 1, 2, 3!

What it takes:
- Pencil
- Piece of paper

It's only three lines long, and it doesn't take many words to write this type of Japanese poetry that describes something you'd see in nature. It's called Haiku, and to get started all you need to do is picture something in your "mind's eye" (in your thoughts) that has to do with nature. There's a recipe that you have to follow, and since each poem is only three lines long you can write several poems in a short time.

The first line is five syllables (sounds you hear in a word); the second line is seven syllables; and the third line is just five syllables. You could picture a waterfall, trees, a rippling brook, waves crashing in the ocean, wind, flowers, birds, and maybe even a snow-covered mountain. Don't forget the little forest animals, or even jungle cats. To get you started, here is a Haiku poem:

> Gen/tle bree/zes blow (5 syllables or sounds)
> Through fields of gol/den pop/pies (7 syllables)
> Wav/ing in the sun (5 syllables)

Are you ready to try on your own? Create several of these. How about one for each season or one for each holiday?

51. FOR BOOKWORMS ONLY

 The plan: Make a bookmark that only a true bookworm will love!

What it takes:
- Ruler
- Pencil
- Scissors
- File folder or colored report folder
- Colored marking pens or crayons

Use your ruler and a pencil to mark off a rectangle four by six inches on one side of a file or report folder, or draw an unusual shape about the same size with curving sides or rounded edges. Cut out your bookmark, and then decorate it with marking pens or crayons.

You may want to personalize your bookmark by printing your name in bold balloon or bubbly letters starting at the top and writing one letter after the other all the way to the bottom. Color the letters in with marking pens or crayons, or maybe you'd like the letters better just outlined. How about a theme for your bookmark? Sports? Nature? Monsters? Don't forget to decorate both sides!

52. YOU AND THE BEANSTALK

 The plan: Plant dried beans in a wet sponge and watch them sprout!

What it takes:
- Old plastic container
- Permanent marking pen
- Dried beans (not green)
- Old sponge
- Water

Write today's date on the outside of the old container with a permanent marking pen. Soak the sponge in water, and put it in the plastic container. Push a few dried beans down into the sponge. Put a little water in the plastic container, but do not let the water cover the sponge. Set the container in a place where it will get plenty of light.

Now you have to wait, watch, and water. The sponge should be kept damp for several days. See how long it takes for the beans to sprout.

53. NUMBER MAZE

 **The plan: Draw lines between the identical numbers
without crossing lines already made.**

What it takes:
- Piece of paper
- Pencil

Write numbers from one to twenty, scattering them all over the whole paper. On the same piece of paper write the numbers from one to twenty again, and scatter them all over the whole paper. Do not put the same numbers near each other.

Now draw a line between the two identical numbers. Here's the catch: *The lines may never cross each other.* When you match the two twentys you will have met quite a challenge! You will understand why this is called Number Maze!

54. RATTLE THOSE ROCKS

 The plan: Create a colorful rattle using a detergent bottle!

What it takes:
- 15 pebbles or dried beans
- Empty plastic detergent bottle
- Permanent colored marking pens

Collect about fifteen pebbles from your yard or use dried beans. Place them in an empty plastic detergent bottle and replace the lid. Decorate the plastic bottle with colored marking pens. Next time your favorite tune is played, you can Rattle Those Rocks!

55. YOU NAME IT

 The plan: Write your name over and over until it turns into an exciting piece of name art!

What it takes:
• Pencil
• Drawing paper
• Black fine-tip marking pen

Write or print your name with a pencil on the drawing paper. Now write it again and again, curving it around, turning corners, crossing over, going up and down, until you've made an interesting design. Try to keep your writing all the same size, but go anywhere on the paper you'd like. You can use your entire name, or just your first or last name. When you finish the design, use a black fine-tip marking pen to go over all the letters, and you'll see that you've created quite a standout design!

56. PENCIL TOP

 The plan: Build a spinning top with a pencil and a round piece of poster board!

What it takes:
• Cup
• Piece of poster board
• Short pencil
• Ruler
• Colored marking pens or crayons
• Scissors

Place a cup upside down on a piece of poster board. Draw a circle by tracing around the cup with the short pencil. Use the ruler to divide the circle into four sections. Color each section differently with colored marking pens or crayons. Cut the circle out. Now push the short pencil through the middle of the circle. Your colorful Pencil Top is ready to spin when you give it a twist of your hand and wrist.

57. TOOTSIE TRICKS

 The plan: Your toes can do more than you think when you do these tootsie tricks!

What it takes:
- Your toes
- Washcloth
- Plastic cup or bowl
- 5 marbles

You'll be amazed at how good your toes are going to get after you practice these quick little exercises. Place a washcloth on the floor, and put your foot in the center. Now curl your toes, and try to pick up the washcloth with your toes. No hands allowed! If you can't do it the first time, keep trying, and when you get toe-terrific with one foot, try the other.

When you've mastered the washcloth trick, you're ready to take on the marbles! All you do is place five marbles on the floor along with a plastic bowl or cup. Now try to pick up the marbles, one at a time, with your toes. You can guess what comes next. You're absolutely right if you knew all along that you'd have to drop the marbles into the bowl. When you're an expert with the marbles, you can definitely go on to bigger and better things. How about pens and pencils?

58. STRIKE

 The plan: Roll tennis balls at empty cans for a good bowling game!

What it takes:
- Cardboard box
- 10 empty soup cans, other cans, or paper cups
- 1 tennis ball

Find a long, flat space at least six feet long, either on the floor or a smooth piece of cement outdoors. Be sure there's nothing breakable around. This flat space is your bowling alley. Open the cardboard box, and place it at one end of your bowling alley with the open side toward you.

The ten empty cans or cups are the bowling "pins." Place the cans or cups just in front of the open box in a triangle shape. You will have four rows of cans or cups: one will be the first row closest to you; two in the second row; three in the third row; and four in the fourth row.

Walk away from the box and the cans or cups to the opposite end of your bowling alley. Now try your luck. Aim the tennis ball right at the "pins" and roll away. Good for you if you got a strike! That means you knocked all the "pins" down with one try.

59. MINI SANDWICHES

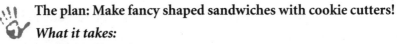 **The plan: Make fancy shaped sandwiches with cookie cutters!**
What it takes:
- 2 slices of bread
- Plate
- Favorite sandwich filling (bologna, cheese, peanut butter, tuna)
- Spatula
- Small cookie cutter

Wash your hands thoroughly with soap and water. Place two slices of bread on a plate. With the spatula cover one slice of bread with sandwich filling, and place the other slice of bread on top. Yum! It looks good enough to eat right now, but it gets even better. Look carefully at the sandwich, and measure with the cookie cutter to see if there is room for two, or only one, shape. If there's room for two, make sure you leave enough space on your sandwich for both cuts.

Press the cookie cutter into the sandwich, cutting all the way through, and gently pull the cutter away. Sometimes the little sandwich will stick inside the cutter, so you will have to gently pull it out with the tip of the spatula. Make as many Mini Sandwiches as you can. Eat and enjoy! The leftover scraps make good snacks for the birds.

60. SIT AND REACH

 The plan: Find out how flexible you are by doing this simple exercise!

What it takes:
- Spoon
- Measuring tape or yardstick
- Pencil
- Piece of paper

Basketball players, hockey players, baseball players, and just about all athletes need to easily bend, stretch, and reach. Find out how flexible you are right now, and then keep practicing until you see some real improvement.

Locate an empty wall in your house and sit down, with your back against the wall and your legs out straight in front of you. Now all you have to do is hold your arms straight out in front of you like you're trying to touch your toes and see how far you can reach. Can you *almost* touch your toes? Maybe you already *can* touch your toes. Do it slowly, no jerking or quick moves, and always stop when you begin to feel a "pull" in your muscles.

Now place a spoon on the floor across the spot where you've been able to reach. Measure the distance from the wall to the spoon with your measuring tape or yardstick, and record it on your paper with a pencil. Sit down and try again.

You're going to be amazed at how flexible you'll become after doing this simple little exercise for several days. How about weeks? Keep a record, and watch how you'll improve.

61. THANK YOU VERY MUCH

 The plan: Write and send thank-you notes to helpful people!

What it takes:
- Writing paper
- Pencil
- Envelopes
- Stamp, if note is mailed

Thank you very much are kind words that everyone likes to hear. Mom, Dad, sister, brother, teacher, doctor, dentist, or your best friend would love to get a "thanks" from you. All it takes is some writing paper, a pencil, and a little imagination. You might write, "Thank you for the good dinner tonight. It was my favorite!" You might even let the dentist know you were glad to get your teeth fixed. It won't take long to write a few words, put the note in an envelope, and take it to the right person. Maybe you'll have to address and stamp the envelope if it has to be mailed. Make someone happy. Write right away.

62. BROOM HOCKEY

 The plan: Play solo hockey using a broom and an old, rolled-up stocking!

What it takes:
- 1 rolled-up old sock
- Chair with legs
- Broom

Find an old sock, and roll it into a ball. Turn the top over the rolled-up part so it won't come undone. Now clear some space in a room. Make certain everything is put safely away because this game can get a little wild.

Place a chair with visible legs at one end of the room. Grab your broom, and walk as far away from the chair as you can get. Put the rolled-up sock on the floor and give it a swish with the broom. It's supposed to land right under the chair legs. What kind of shot are you? Try it again. You might be another Wayne Gretzky.

63. SWING AND PUTT

The plan: Putt tennis balls into plastic jars or large tin cans!

What it takes:
- 4 large plastic containers or 4 large tin cans
- 4 tennis balls
- Yardstick

Here's your chance to become a PGA or LPGA champion by learning the art of putting. First make sure there's plenty of clear room on the floor. Place the plastic containers or tin cans on their sides with the open end toward you. Walk about five big steps away from the containers, and place the tennis balls on the floor.

Here comes the challenge! With the end of the yardstick, gently tap a tennis ball toward the containers or cans. If you're a good golfer the tennis ball will gently roll right into the targets. Putt all four balls, and see how many make their mark.

64. SWEET CRYSTALS

The plan: Grow crystals, and watch a liquid change into a solid before your very eyes!

What it takes:
- ½ cup sugar
- 1-quart glass jar
- Water
- Spoon
- 12-inch piece of cotton string
- Nail or pencil
- Paper clip

Put ½ cup sugar in a jar, and add hot tap water until the water level is about two inches above the sugar. Stir the mixture until the sugar is dissolved. Tie one end of the string to the center of a long nail or pencil. Tie the other end to a paper clip so it will stay down in the liquid. Drop the end with the paper clip into the jar so that it touches the bottom.

Place the nail or pencil across the top of the jar, and adjust the string with the paper clip to be sure it hangs down into the liquid and touches the bottom of the jar. You now have everything in place to grow sugar crystals. Place the jar on a table or shelf, and in two to three days tiny crystals will begin to form. The longer you leave the string in the sugar water, the more crystals you can grow.

65. NUTTY BOATS

 The plan: Make seaworthy tiny sailing boats out of walnut shell halves!

What it takes:

- Walnuts shell halves
- Modeling clay
- Construction paper
- Pencil
- Scissors
- Toothpicks

These little boats can really float, and here's what you do to get them ready for any trip. First, take a walnut shell half and make sure the nutty part is all cleaned out. Press a little bit of clay into the bottom of the shell. Use a pencil to draw a "sail" on the paper that measures about two inches square, and cut it out. Attach the "sail" to a toothpick by sticking the toothpick in through the bottom of the paper sail and out through the top. Place the toothpick mast into the clay.

These are so easy to make that you may end up making a whole fleet. Float them in the bathtub when you take a bath. A kitchen sink filled with water makes a great lake!

66. SOCK TOSS ACROSS

 The plan: Toss rolled stockings into different size containers!

What it takes:

- 8 open containers of different sizes (shoe boxes, mixing bowls, plastic bowls)
- 8 socks with the cuff rolled over the rolled-up foot
- Timer or watch that displays seconds

Line up eight open containers across one end of the room. Practice throwing rolled-up socks into the containers from a distance of three big steps. Move back two more steps. Practice from this distance. Now set the timer for one minute or use a watch that displays seconds. Try to toss a sock into each of the eight containers before the timer dings. If you can do it in one minute, you are ready to move back another two steps and try your luck from that distance.

Your skill as a tosser will certainly improve if you practice Sock Toss Across.

67. GREAT FOR GRAPES

 The plan: Mix up a wonderful yogurt fruit dip!

What it takes:

- 1 cup plain yogurt
- Small mixing bowl
- 2 tablespoons brown sugar
- Mixing spoon
- Grapes or other fruit

This recipe is quick and easy. Wash your hands with soap and water. Get out all of *What it takes*. Place the yogurt into a mixing bowl. Add the brown sugar to the yogurt and stir until the sugar is dissolved. Wash the grapes or other dipping fruit.

You'll love this tangy but sweet fruit dip. It's especially great for dipping grapes. Don't forget to clean up the kitchen before you enjoy this luscious treat!

68. IS IT A GHOST?

 The plan: Make a whimsical Halloween ghost that's way too cute to be scary!

What it takes:
- Facial tissue or a paper napkin
- White paper napkin, paper towel, or a napkin-size square of white fabric
- A 12-inch piece of string or yarn
- Scissors
- Black marking pen or crayon

Be ready for those trick-or-treaters on October 31 this year! This little ghost may not scare anyone, but it will help get you in the Halloween mood, and you can make it nearly as fast as you can say, *"one . . . two . . . three . . . BOO!"*

Make a round "ball" with a tissue or paper napkin by scrunching it up in your hand. Next, place an unfolded napkin, paper towel, or fabric square over the top of the "ball" and pinch it tight under the ball. This is your ghost's head, and the rest of the napkin or fabric hanging down is the body. Cut a piece of string or yarn, tie it around the "neck," and use a black marker to make two big eyes if your ghost is made of fabric. Use a crayon if you've used a paper napkin or tissue. Do you want your ghost to have a mouth? A straight black line or even a zigzag line can make a ghost's face look mighty scary. Use the neck string to hang your ghost from a doorway (with help from an adult and a pushpin.) Something to think about: How about making *lots* of ghosts of different sizes?

69. CLIP ART

 The plan: Create the biggest, funniest, silliest, prettiest pictures you want, anywhere!

What it takes:
- A big handful of paper clips (colored ones are great)
- Any flat surface

Take a handful of paper clips and then find the perfect spot for your "clip" creation. Choose any flat surface, like the floor or a tabletop. Make yourself comfortable, then start thinking about what you would like to "draw" with your paper clips. For instance, paper clip boats and planes look great; so do houses with trees. Don't forget the chimney with paper clip smoke winding out of it. Paper clip animals such as elephants with long trunks or giraffes with long necks have distinct features that are easy to show. How about considering a paper clip outline of your state?

Now that your imagination is working, you can begin by making an outline of the object you're thinking of, laying the paper clips end-to-end on your flat surface. Does the outline look like the picture in your mind? You may then wish to fill in parts of your paper Clip Art with additional paper clips inside the outline drawing. This will make the object look more solid.

You can "draw" almost anything with your paper clips, and best of all, if you don't like what you did, there's nothing to erase—just grab them up and start again!

70. WHAT'S IN YOUR NAME?

 The plan: Write all the words you can think of that begin with the letters of your name!

What it takes:
- Piece of lined paper
- Pencil

Use a pencil to write your name down the lines of a piece of lined paper with one letter on each line. Now think of all the words or phrases that describe you, beginning with each letter of your name. If your name is CHRIS you could write the word "cheerful" next to the letter C. How about using "helpful" for the letter H, and "really great" for the letter R (don't forget that you can use more than one word). The letter I could be "intelligent" and the letter S is for "super."

Now it's your turn to see what great words you can think of to describe yourself or a family member or friend.

71. FANCY FISH

 The plan: Make a fish from a paper plate!

What it takes:
- 1 paper plate
- Scissors
- White glue
- Crayons

Cut out a triangle shape that looks like a piece of pizza from the paper plate. Glue the piece-of-pizza shape on the opposite side of the plate to form a tail with the point of the triangle glued onto the plate. Color a fish eye on top of the triangular, cutout mouth, and then color fancy fish scales and fancy fish gills all over the plate and tail.

72. ALL IN A DAY'S WORK

 The plan: See how many different jobs you can write down in five minutes!

What it takes:
- Lined paper
- Pencil
- Watch or clock

Butcher, baker, candlestick maker are three, but there must be thousands of other jobs that people go to every day. Find out how good you are at coming up with job names in five minutes. Get your pencil and paper ready to job search. Write down as many jobs as you can. Check the timer on a watch or clock. Lawyer, fireman, teacher, go!

73. INITIAL ART

 The plan: Turn the first letter of your name into an initial work of art!

What it takes:
- White drawing paper
- Pencil
- Colored marking pens or crayons

Use a pencil to draw the first letter of your name as large and as fat as you can on the white drawing paper. Outline it with a marking pen. Now think about all of the things that tell something about you and what you like to do. Do you play an instrument, play sports, or love to do math? What are some of your favorite foods? With your pencil, decorate your initial with some of your favorite things.

When you've finished with decorating your initial, brighten it up with your colored marking pens or crayons. Do you have enough ideas left over to do the first initial in your last name?

74. WALK TALL WITH TOES STRAIGHT

 The plan: Walk around the room with a book on your head and pennies on your toes!

What it takes:
- 2 pennies
- 1 thick book

Improve your posture and your walk by practicing this exercise each day. Take off your shoes and socks and set one penny on each big toenail. Now grab your thick book and balance it on top of your head and go for a walk. You'll have lots of fun trying to keep the pennies and book in place. With a book on your head and a penny on your toe, you will look funny wherever you go!

75. SQUEEZE THOSE TOES

 The plan: Place pennies between your toes and walk around the room!

What it takes:
- 8 pennies
- Your own bare feet

Here is a great activity to keep your toes and feet in good condition. All you have to do is take off your shoes and socks and place a penny between your toes on both feet (four pennies for each foot). Now go for a walk around the room. You'll have to squeeze your toes pretty tight to keep the pennies in place. If you're able to walk around one room, how about walking around the whole house? Exercise your toes this way each day, and you'll soon have the tightest toe squeeze in town.

FIFTEEN-MINUTE ACTIVITIES

Can you even imagine constructing a work of art out of frozen peas and toothpicks? If you have **Fifteen Minutes** with nothing to do and not a playmate in sight, keep reading, and get set for a creative first! If this little adventure reminds you that you're hungry, try another **Fifteen-Minute Activity** that will tempt those taste buds. Clue: It's **Banana Crunchies** time!

76. PLEASE PASS THE PEAS

 The plan: Use frozen peas and toothpicks to make a super sculpture!

What it takes:
- Package of frozen peas
- Round toothpicks

Create a sculpture by sticking toothpicks into frozen peas. You can build your structure up or down, out and in, and any way you'd like. Experiment: When the peas dry out they will harden and keep the toothpicks in place. Pass the peas, please!

77. JUMP-ROPE JINGLES

 The plan: Make up your own jump-rope jingles, and then see if they help you jump!

What it takes:
- Jump rope
- Pencil
- Piece of paper

You probably already know some jump-rope chants or jingles, but now why don't you see if you can make up your own. You may even want to share them with a friend. Maybe you could even start a jump-rope jingle book where you and your friends write your own original jingle creations and then get together to try them out. Warm up by jumping the rope a few times to get the feel of the rhythm of jumping. Try a double jump every time the rope turns, and then try a single jump. Here's an old tried-and-true jingle to get you started.

> Mama, Mama, I am sick
> Send for the doctor, quick, quick, quick!
> Mama called the doctor
> The doctor called the nurse
> The nurse called the lady with the alligator purse
> How many pills did the lady bring?
> 1, 2, 3, ——— (count, and jump until you miss)

Now pick up a pencil and paper and become a jump-rope jingle creator!

78. FINGER TALKING

 The plan: Make animals, people, scary monsters, or just plain silly folk with a thumbprint!

What it takes:
- Tempera paint or an ink pad
- Paper plate
- Plain white paper
- Black fine-tip marking pen
- One clean thumb

You'll be able to make some terrific characters in no time flat, and the more you make the better they'll get. If you're using tempera paint, pour a small amount, about the size of a quarter, onto a paper plate. If you're using an ink pad, you're ready to begin.

Press your thumb into the paint or ink pad, and then carefully press it onto the paper. That's it! You may be able to make more than one print before you have to put more ink or paint on your thumb again. If you're using paint, you may want to make a thumbprint or two on another piece of paper to get rid of the excess paint before you do the real thing on the good paper.

Try making a T-Rex by using three or four thumbprints for the body and another for the head. You could even use a little finger "pinkie" print for his tail sections. Use thumbprints for faces, and you can even connect prints to make entire people or animals.

Next, wipe your thumb clean, pick up your marking pen, and you're all set to add the details. Add eyes, noses, and other body parts with your pen. How would you make a tiger? You can make great stripes with your fine-tip marker, and don't forget the whiskers!

79. HOLIDAY SCRAMBLE

 The plan: Make up as many words as you can by using the names of your favorite holidays!

What it takes:
• Piece of paper
• Pencil

Cozy up to a table, take your paper and pencil, and write down the name of a favorite holiday in big letters across the top of your paper. Now all you have to do is use any of the letters in any order to make up a word. You decide whether or not you want to include two-letter words like "in."

For example, how many words can you make out of *Thanksgiving* using only the letters in the word? There's only one *H*, so you can use this letter only once. Luckily, you can use the letter *I* two times, since there are two of this letter.

Write down all the words you can think of and then go back and count them. Now pick another holiday, and see how many words you can find in this new word or words. In the word *Thanksgiving* did you find *tank, skin, van,* and *hang*? How many words do you think you can make out of the *Fourth of July? Rosh Hashanah?*

80. WATERY WATERCOLORS

 The plan: Use wet drawing paper and paints to watercolor a masterpiece!

What it takes:
• Pencil
• White drawing paper
• Old newspapers
• Paintbrush
• Watercolor or tempera paints
• Bowl of water for the paint
• Fine-point marking pen

Lightly sketch a scene on a piece of white drawing paper with a pencil. Now hold the paper under a dripping water faucet for a few seconds. Let the water drip off the paper into the sink, and when the dripping stops, place the wet paper on a piece of newspaper. Use your paintbrush and paints to brush on areas of color. Don't worry about the details. They'll come later.

You may want a blue sky, a blue-green pond, some green fir trees, and purple mountains in the background. The colors will all blend together on the wet paper. Wait until the painting dries, and then use a fine marking pen to add the details such as the trunk and branches on a tree, grass around a pond, cloud shapes in the sky, and mountain peaks. Your picture will look like a true watercolor!

81. HOMEMADE SQUISHY PUTTY

 The plan: Make squishy putty just like you buy in the store, and make lots of great shapes!

What it takes:
- 1 cup white glue
- 1½ cup liquid starch
- Bowl
- Spoon
- Tempera paint or food coloring
- Plastic wrap

Mix the glue and the starch together in a bowl with the spoon. Add a little tempera or a few drops of food coloring if you want to have colored putty. Cover the bowl with plastic wrap, and let it stand overnight. You can make more than one recipe with different colors if you'd like.

The next day pour off any liquid that is standing on top of the glue-starch mixture. Use your hands to work the putty back and forth until it feels like clay. You can now roll it, pound it, or use it just like clay to turn it into wonderful shapes.

82. SPIFFY SOCKS

 The plan: Spiff up a pair of plain old socks with neat designs and pictures!

What it takes:
- Pencil
- Piece of paper
- One pair of light-colored crew socks or ankle socks
- Permanent felt-tip pens in different colors

Decide on a design or a picture. Keep it simple. Try out your ideas with a pencil and paper first. If you're using crew socks that can be turned down for a cuff, turn them down before you begin your artwork. If you're using the shorter ankle socks, you can draw right on the band at the top.

When you are ready, use your pencil and then your pens to draw one design, and then repeat the same design around the entire cuff or band. Use a darker pen for outlining, and color in spots that you want solid. Hearts, flowers, butterflies, and polka dots would look great, and so would footballs, soccer balls, letters of the alphabet, and even names such as your own name or the name of your school. Your old socks will be spiffed up in no time!

83. YOUR OWN NAME POEM

 The plan: Use your whole name to make a poem about YOU **or anything you'd like!**

What it takes:
- Lined notebook paper
- Pencil

Take a break, and sit at a table with a paper and pencil and lots of great ideas. Write the letters of your name down the left-hand side of the paper with one letter on each line. Good. Now start thinking of a word that begins with each letter of your name. Remember, this is a type of poem, but it doesn't have to rhyme.

Check out this example, and then you're on your own to making your name poetic. How about using the names of all of your family members, including the dog or cat!

Little
Islands
Stand
Alone

When
Earthquakes
And
Volcanoes
Erupt
Regularly

84. PRESSED SPRING FLOWERS

 The plan: Gather flowers and leaves for a pressed artwork you can make next month!

What it takes:

- Scissors
- Flowers and leaves
- File folder or manila envelope
- Waxed paper
- Heavy books
- Heavy white or cream-colored paper
- White glue

Do this activity in the spring or summer when there are lots of flowers blooming. Carefully snip off some flowers and leaves with scissors, and place them in a folder or large envelope as you walk through your yard or garden. When you go back inside, remove the flowers and leaves from the folder or envelope, place them between two pieces of waxed paper, and then insert the whole thing between the pages of a heavy book. You may want to place another heavy book on top of the one with the flowers.

It will take about four weeks to have your blossoms and leaves pressed and ready for a picture. When they're flat and no longer moist, gently place them in a dry container such as a box until you're ready to make a pressed flower picture. To make your picture, simply glue the flower petals and leaves on a piece of heavy white or cream-colored paper, and you'll have a picture worth framing!

85. BANANA CRUNCHIES

 The plan: Cover sliced bananas with crunchy wafer crumbs to make a tasty finger treat!

What it takes:
- Vanilla or chocolate wafer cookies
- 1-gallon size reclosable plastic bag
- Table knife
- Dinner plate
- Cookie sheet
- Bananas
- Rolling pin
- Waxed paper

Begin by washing your hands with soap and water. Then place about ten vanilla or chocolate wafers in a plastic bag, and use a rolling pin to roll the cookies until they turn into crumbs. Place the crumbs on a cookie sheet. Repeat the process with ten more cookies. Next, peel a banana and use a table knife to cut it into one-inch-thick slices. Place the banana slices in the crumbs, and use your hands to cover the banana pieces completely, turning them over. Remove the coated banana slices from the crumbs, and place them on a plate covered with waxed paper. Place the banana crunchies in the refrigerator until the crumbs really stick to the banana slices, if you haven't sampled them all first!

86. MARBLE MURAL

 The plan: A marble on the loose can make some of the most interesting designs imaginable!

What it takes:
- Tempera paint
- Bowls for as many colors of paint as you'll use
- White construction paper
- Shallow box, such as a shirt box

- Marbles
- Spoon for each bowl
- Large bowl of water
- Paper towels

Place small amounts of different colored paints in separate bowls. Next place a piece of paper in the bottom of a box. Put a marble in each bowl of paint, and let it roll around. Use a spoon to remove one of the marbles, and place it on the paper in the box. Continue to remove the other marbles from the bowls one at a time, using a different spoon for each color. Place them on the paper in the box.

Now pick up the box, and gently move it so that the marbles roll around from one side to the other, through the middle and anywhere they'd like to go. When you've achieved an interesting design, take the marbles out with a spoon and wash them off in the bowl of water. Use the paper towel to dry them off and clean the area. Let the paper dry, and see just how creative marbles on the loose can be!

87. SNOW SCENE IN A JAR

 The plan: Make a scene in a jar that turns into a snowstorm when you shake it up!

What it takes:
- Tiny plastic figures such as a snowman, trees, animals
- Baby food jar or small glass jar with a lid
- Epoxy glue
- Water
- White glitter or moth flakes

Glue some tiny figures onto the inside lid of a baby food jar, or any small glass jar, with epoxy glue. Let this dry. Next, fill the jar up almost to the top with water, and add some moth flakes or white glitter, or a little of both. This will be the snow. Put some of the epoxy glue around the inside rim of the jar lid, and screw the lid on tightly to seal it. To produce your own snowstorm in a jar, turn the jar upside down and gently shake it. How long do you think it will take for the snow to settle to the ground?

88. STRING PAINTING

 The plan: A piece of string that's dipped into paint will produce an amazing picture!

What it takes:
- Drawing paper
- 5 colors of tempera paint
- 5 shallow dishes
- 5 pieces of string at least 12 inches long

Fold a piece of drawing paper in half, and then open it up. Pour small amounts of five different colors of tempera paint into five separate dishes. Dip one piece of string into one of the colors, holding on to the dry end. Pull the string out of the dish and place it on the paper. Hold the dry end at the edge of the paper. Keep holding on to the string and fold the paper over it, using your other hand. Now press down on the paper and pull the string out. Open the paper.

Dip all the other pieces of string one at a time into different colors. Use a clean piece of string for each color. Open the paper each time, and place the string inside. Fold the paper over, and pull the string out.

You can make even more interesting effects by pulling the string sideways around the paper or pulling it out a different side than the one before. Open the paper, and let the paint dry for an amazingly different kind of picture.

89. VEGGIE DECORATING

 The plan: Use unusual vegetables like radishes and zucchini to make crazy characters!

What it takes:
- Cucumbers, carrots, radishes, zucchini, or *any* kind of squash
- Little bits and pieces of other things to eat, such as corn kernels, raisins, shelled nuts, tops of celery, pretzel pieces
- Bits of fabric scraps, sequins, buttons, ribbon, pipe cleaners
- Scissors
- White glue
- Straight pins

Pumpkins aren't the only vegetable that can be decorated. Try your hand with other veggies right out of the vegetable drawer in your refrigerator. Just make sure you have a grown-up's okay first! Use your wildest imagination to make some crazy characters. You can glue on or pin on bits and pieces of things such as buttons and sequins, or just about anything that will help your veggie look like a person or even a monster. How about celery leaves for some kind of a wild hairdo? Pretzel sticks placed just right will give any zucchini head a scared look, or even make it look like a porcupine. Just think of what you can do with popcorn kernels. Maybe a silly grin?

90. BEANBAG SOCK GAMES

 The plan: Make your own beanbags with a pair of old socks!

What it takes:
- Pair of old socks (no holes in the toes!)
- Dry beans or rice
- Rubber bands or pieces of string
- Cooking pans

Put a handful of beans or rice in the toe and foot part of an old sock. Tie off the sock above the beans with a piece of string or a rubber band wrapped around tight so the beans or rice won't spill out. Now you can invent any number of beanbag games. For a starter, try tossing a beanbag into a pan a few steps away from you. Can you keep backing up and still hit the pan?

You can also line up three pots or pans touching each other right in a row, with the first pan being worth twenty points, the second one worth ten points, and the third one worth five points. See how many points you can accumulate in ten tosses. How many more beanbag games can you invent?

91. POPCORN POPPING!

 The plan: Create a blooming tree out of popcorn that looks just like blossoms!

What it takes:
- Pencil
- Light blue, brown, and green construction paper
- Scissors
- White glue
- Popped popcorn

Take your pencil and draw the trunk and branches of a tree on a piece of brown construction paper. Cut it out so that it fits on the piece of light blue construction paper. Glue the tree in place; then cut out lots of little green construction paper leaves. Glue them onto the tree branches. Glue pieces of popcorn on the tree near all of the leaves. Use two or three pieces of popcorn for some branches, and only one piece for others. Doesn't this look just like a real fruit tree that you see blossoming every spring?

92. ONE, TWO, THREE O'LEARY

 The plan: Invent your own jingles to this ball-bouncing activity that's been done for years!

What it takes:
- Pencil
- Piece of paper
- Rubber ball

This is a ball-bouncing game that kids have done way before Grandma's time, and it's still loads of fun. Practice bouncing a ball and saying:

> One, two, three O'Leary
> Four, five, six, O'Leary
> Seven, eight, nine, O'Leary
> Ten, O'Leary Boys! (Or Girls!)

Every time you say, "O'Leary," swing your right or left leg over the ball without touching it, and then continue bouncing. When you get really good, you can spin around on the "O'Leary," or clap your hands in back *and* in front of yourself. You can also raise both arms and quickly clap your hands together three times over your head on the "O'Leary." When you say, "Ten, O'Leary Boys!" bounce the ball two times and catch it. Then you get to start all over.

Think up your own rhymes and write them with a pencil on a piece of paper. How about something like:

One, two, three O'Leary
I think you are scary
You look like a berry
So never ask me to marry!

93. THE BLOB

 The plan: You can mix it, blend it, and then smoosh it together between a folded paper!

What it takes:
- Old newspaper
- White construction paper
- Paintbrush
- Tempera paint
- Scissors

Cover your work area with old newspapers. Then place all of *What it takes* on top of the newspaper. Now fold a piece of white paper in half, and open it up. Use your brush to drop globs of paint onto the fold line. Use different colors, and you can even drop them right on top of each other. Make some extra globs on other parts of the paper. Fold the paper back together just like you did the first time. Now use your hand and fingers to rub the top of the folded paper, pushing the paint on the inside of the paper out toward the edges. Open up the paper to see what a surprise picture you've made. When it's dry, cut out shapes such as a butterfly, flowers, or anything else that's colorful.

94. GRAPE BANANASICLE

 The plan: Freeze white grape juice, mashed banana, and yogurt for a delicious treat!

What it takes:

- Mixing bowl
- 1 soft banana
- Fork
- Measuring spoons
- 3 tablespoons white grape juice concentrate
- Measuring cup
- ½ cup plain yogurt
- 2 small paper cups
- Aluminum foil
- 2 popsicle sticks

Wash your hands with soap and water. Get out all of *What it takes.* In a mixing bowl mash one soft banana with a fork. Stir in three tablespoons of white grape juice concentrate and ½ cup of plain yogurt. Divide the mixture into two small paper cups.

Cover the top of each cup with aluminum foil. Gently insert a popsicle stick in the middle of each cup, through the aluminum foil. The aluminum foil will keep the popsicle stick from falling over.

Freeze your Grape Bananasicles. They should be ready to eat in about four hours.

95. SILLY ZOO TIME

 The plan: Combine two different animals to make up your own original species!

What it takes:

- Pencil
- White drawing paper
- Colored marking pens or crayons

There really is such an animal as a liger, which is a combination of a lion and a tiger, but can you think up some other combinations for a silly zoo? What about combining a rhinoceros and an elephant? Would it be called a rhinophant? Of course, you'd have to draw one so people would believe you. Such a silly zoo animal would surely have a trunk, but what about a horn like rhinos have?

Get your zookeeper thinking cap on and see how many silly zoo animals you can invent and name. Use your pencil to make an illustration of your animal on a piece of paper. Color it in, and write its name below the drawing. What in the world would a bearaccoon look like? Can you draw one?

96. RUBBERY FUN

 The plan: Use rubber cement to paint a picture that will appear when you rub the glue off!

What it takes:
- Pencil
- White drawing paper
- Rubber cement glue with the brush attached to the lid
- Watercolors or tempera paint
- Paintbrush

Sketch a simple design or picture with a pencil on a piece of drawing paper. Use rubber cement to "paint" your picture. Keep the objects large and don't use much detail. When the rubber cement is dry, all you have to do is brush over the entire paper, glue and all, with some tempera or watercolors.

When the paper is dry gently rub off the rubber cement, and you'll see a great picture. Try simple subjects like a snowman, a tree, a leaf design, a polar bear, rabbit, cat, or other animal. Since the picture will be white when you rub off the rubber cement, think about drawing something that is white in real life.

97. MAY I PLEASE SEE YOUR LICENSE?

 The plan: Create your own special message license plates (U GOT IT)?

What it takes:
- White drawing paper
- Pencil
- Colored marking pens or crayons

Have you noticed some of the unusual messages on license plates attached to the back of cars? Sometimes it's a real challenge trying to figure out what they say, but it's so much fun! How about these for starters? FALLOME (follow me) or URCOOL (you are cool) or RCKNROL (rock 'n' roll).

Try coming up with your own one-of-a-kind catchy license plate design. All you need to do is draw a license plate–shaped rectangle on a plain piece of paper, and add up to seven large, fat letters that give a message. You can even leave out a vowel or two if it still makes sense. You can also leave a space anywhere you'd like.

Don't forget to print the name of your state on your "plate" design along with the year. Next, all you have to do is color in those big letters and you've got yourself a WINNER. Can you think of a license plate using YOUR name? SUPRMAN and RBNHOOD can!

98. NATURE STENCILS

 The plan: Use leaves to stencil a print on paper or note cards, or just about anything!

What it takes:
- Light-colored construction paper
- Leaves from different trees and bushes
- Masking tape or transparent tape
- Tempera paints
- Bowl
- Sponge or a hard-bristle brush

It doesn't have to be fall to make leaf stencils. You can do them on just about anything, anytime, but try your skill on a piece of construction paper first. Then you can fold the paper and make note cards or stationery.

Place one leaf at a time on a piece of paper. You can keep the leaf in place by putting a little rolled-up piece of tape underneath it so that it sticks to the paper. Pour a small amount of paint into a bowl, and then dip a sponge or brush into the paint. Now dab the paint all around the outside edge of your leaf so that the paint is going onto the paper. When the paint is dry, carefully pick up the leaf, and you'll discover a perfect stencil. Do the same thing with other leaves, and you'll have a wonderful print. What are you going to stencil next?

99. VALENTINE BUTTERFLY

 The plan: Turn 3 hearts into a beautiful Valentine butterfly!
What it takes:
- Red, white, pink, or other colors of construction paper
- Pencil
- Scissors
- White glue

Fold a piece of construction paper in half. Draw half a heart, using the fold as the middle. Cut out the half heart and open up your paper. You now have one whole heart and this will be the pattern for the body of a butterfly. Now trace around this heart on another piece of paper so you'll have one without the center fold. Cut it out, and this will be the actual butterfly body.

Next, cut out another heart, only shorter and fatter, on a folded piece of paper just like you did the first one. Use this as a pattern to make two hearts. These two hearts will be the butterfly's wings. To assemble your butterfly, glue the body heart over the pointed ends of the two fatter hearts so that the rounded ends stick out on the sides of the body. Cut out thin paper strips and glue under the body heart at the top for the antennae. Your butterfly is now ready to sit on the leaf of a houseplant!

100. SHOELACES AND SCHMOOLACES

 The plan: Make a "designer" pair of shoelaces for those tennies and tie-on shoes!

What it takes:
- Pair of white shoelaces
- Old newspaper
- Pencil
- Permanent marking pens

If you don't know what a schmoolace is, it's okay, as long as you know what a shoelace is, and of course, you do! For the best-looking shoelaces on the sidewalk, basketball court, or playground, just spread out the two laces on a piece of newspaper.

Next, decide on a simple design that you can easily repeat over and over. Outline the patterns first with a pencil, and then color them in with permanent marking pens until both laces are decorated. Triangles, squares, hearts, footballs, flowers, baseball bats, apples, and anything you'd like will turn those ordinary laces into the jazziest laces ever.

101. PINECONE BIRD FEEDER

 The plan: Cover a pinecone with peanut butter, hang it in a tree, and wait for the birds!

What it takes:
- Yarn or ribbon
- A good-sized pinecone
- Spoon
- Peanut butter
- Pie plate or cake pan
- Birdseed, or bread, cereal, or cracker crumbs

Birds who like to feed from tree branches will love this tasty treat, especially during the winter when food may be hard to find.

First, tie a piece of yarn or a ribbon securely in the end of the pinecone. Use your spoon to spread peanut butter all over the pinecone. Don't forget to push some into the nooks and crannies.

Pour some birdseed or crumbs onto a pie plate or cake pan, and roll the pinecone in the seeds or crumbs until it is covered. You may need to use your hand to pat on some more. Now go outside and find a suitable tree. When an adult can help you, hang your pinecone bird feeder on the end of a branch where the birds will be sure to see it. Calling all birds!

102. RAINY DAY PAINTING

 The plan: Make a *real* watercolor, using raindrops (or a spray bottle if it's sunny)!

What it takes:
- White drawing paper
- Pencil
- Colored washable marking pens or tempera paint
- Paintbrush
- Cup of water to rinse paintbrush
- A rainy day or a spray bottle filled with water

This is a great activity for a rainy day, but you can still do it even when the sun shines! Lightly make a sketch of your choice with a pencil on the white paper. Landscapes, flowers, wildlife, or maybe simple shapes will all work well. Color your picture with paint, or use washable marking pens.

When you're finished, and if it's raining, grab an umbrella and carefully place your picture on the sidewalk or the grass for just a few seconds, until the marking pens or paint begin to run a little. Be careful not to get the painting too wet. Just a few drops will do. If you want to do this on a day when it isn't raining, simply fill a spray bottle with water, take your picture outside, and lightly spray it. Both methods will produce a wonderful, watery watercolor!

103. SQUISHY SLATE

 The plan: Fill a plastic bag with a secret mixture and "feel" your way through a picture!

What it takes:

- Mixing bowl
- 1 cup cornstarch
- 1-gallon-size reclosable plastic bag
- Water
- Tempera paint
- Spoon

Put 1 cup cornstarch into a mixing bowl and add enough water to make a thick "goo." Stir until the mixture is smooth, adding a little more cornstarch or water to get a squishy, gooey mixture. Add a few drops of tempera paint for color, and then spoon about four spoonfuls of the mixture into a reclosable plastic bag. Be sure to get all of the air out of the plastic bag before sealing it.

Smooth out the mixture in the bag by gently moving your fingertips over the bag. Make designs, draw pictures, and have fun "feeling" a picture. When you want to start over, all you have to do is smooth over the plastic bag and your slate is ready for a new design!

104. HAND-CHURNED BUTTER

 The plan: Act like a pioneer and churn your own butter with whipping cream and ice!

What it takes:
- Small glass jar, such as a baby food jar
- About 3 tablespoons whipping cream (heavy cream), unwhipped
- Small bowl
- Large bowl
- Ice cubes
- Spoon

Fill a baby food or a similar size jar almost but not quite half full of whipping cream. Tighten the lid on the jar and shake the jar back and forth in your hand. Trade hands when one hand gets tired!

Shake the jar, and continue shaking until you notice that the cream is beginning to thicken. Take the lid off for a peek to see if the cream is getting thick.

When it's thick enough that it barely shakes, spoon the thickened cream, which is now soft butter, into the small bowl. Now set the bowl of soft butter into a larger bowl of ice. Stir the butter, and then smooth it out with a spoon. The ice will harden the butter, and now all you need is a piece of toast!

105. BRUSH AND SPARKLE

 The plan: Make a picture that sparkles when you add salt and flour to your paint!

What it takes:

- Colored or white construction paper
- Pencil
- 4 bowls
- Teaspoon
- Flour
- Salt
- Tempera paint (at least 4 colors)
- Water
- Paintbrush

Sketch a design or draw a picture with a pencil on a piece of construction paper. Set it aside. Now place the four bowls in front of you and measure one teaspoon of flour and one teaspoon of salt into each of the four bowls. Add a different color of tempera paint to each of the four bowls. Add just enough water so that the paint is thin enough to use with a paintbrush. Stir each one well. Now paint your design or picture on the paper following the sketch you've already made, and be ready for a surprise when it's dry. The salt in the paint mixture will make your picture sparkle!

106. PANTY HOSE PADDLEBALL

 The plan: Mom's old panty hose stretched over a bent coat hanger makes a great paddle!

What it takes:
- 1 wire coat hanger
- Pair of old panty hose
- Scissors
- String
- Craft pom-poms, cotton balls, scrunched balls of paper, blown-up balloon

Bend a wire coat hanger into a diamond shape by pulling the bottom down, and then stretch a panty hose leg over the diamond shape from the bottom up. Cut the rest of the panty hose off at each end, and tie off the ends with pieces of string. Now that you have the paddle, all you need to do is find something to bat up in the air.

Pom-poms, cotton balls, little balls of wadded-up paper, a blown-up balloon, or anything light will make an excellent "ball" for you to try and keep up in the air without it ever touching the ground. You could even make another paddle with the other panty hose leg and another coat hanger so that some other time you and a partner can hit back and forth.

107. FROZEN NANADREAMS

 The plan: Dip bananas in yogurt and crushed cereal; then freeze for a cold treat!

What it takes:
- ½ cup crushed cornflakes or other dry cereal
- Plastic bag (with no holes)
- Rolling pin
- Measuring cup
- Pie tin
- 2 bananas
- Small container of your favorite flavor yogurt
- Plastic wrap

Wash your hands with soap and water. Get out all of *What it takes*. Put two handfuls of cornflakes or other dry cereal into the bottom of a plastic bag. Crush the cereal by rolling the rolling pin over the bag. Shake the cereal to the bottom of the bag after each roll so it won't spill out. Measure out ½ cup of the crushed cereal, and put it into a pie tin. Set it aside.

Peel the bananas. Dip one whole banana at a time into your favorite flavor of yogurt, holding it with your fingers. You can dip right in the yogurt container, first one half and then the other. Don't lick your fingers!

Roll the bananas in the crushed cereal until they are completely coated with crumbs. Leave the bananas in the pie tin, and cover them with plastic wrap. Put the bananas in the freezer, and in about three hours your Frozen Nanadreams will be a cold treat.

108. STRING ALONG DESIGNS

 The plan: Use string tied to a block of wood to make first-rate prints!

What it takes:
- Small block of wood about the size of your hand
- String
- Scissors
- Tempera paint
- Shallow pan
- White or light-colored construction paper

Hold a block of wood in one hand; using your other hand, wrap string around the block of wood. Don't wrap the string over and over in one spot. Spread it out. Tie it off. Pour a small amount of tempera paint into a pan, and press the block, any string side down, into the paint. To make a print, place the string side covered with paint on a piece of paper and press down. Make your string designs in different directions, and you may even want to change colors.

109. PAINT YOUR FACE!

 The plan: You'll put on a festive look when you use wash-off paints to decorate your face!

What it takes:
- Mirror
- Water
- Paintbrushes of different sizes
- Watercolors
- Washcloth or paper towels
- Tissue
- Soap or cleansing cream

You can celebrate a holiday by painting your own face with some dandy designs that show the day you're celebrating. Maybe a shamrock for St. Patrick's Day or a holly leaf and berries for Christmas would be eye-catching. You could even make designs that go with any time of the year, such as stars, flowers, rainbows, animals, hearts, and lightning bolts. You could even write words on your face!

Sit down in front of a mirror. Now moisten a paintbrush and dip it into the paint. Try the color out on your arm or hand to see if it's dark enough. Make a design on your face with the paint and brush. If you're not happy with how it looks, all you need to do is wipe it off with a moistened washcloth or paper towel.

Experiment with a design or two until you decide on the perfect face painting. The paint will wash off easily with a washcloth or paper towel moistened with water and a little soap. If mom wouldn't mind, maybe you could borrow some of her cleansing cream to wipe on your face and then wipe off with a tissue. Be sure to rinse with warm water and a washcloth.

110. PAPER PLATE YARN WREATH

 The plan: Make a Happy Holiday wreath by wrapping green yarn over a paper plate!

What it takes:

- Paper plate
- Scissors
- Ball or skein of green yarn
- Transparent tape
- Red ball fringe or red pom-poms
- Red ribbon for a bow

Cut the center out of a paper plate and throw the center piece away. Tape the end of the yarn to the back of the paper plate hoop that is going to be your wreath, and wrap the yarn around and around through the rim of the plate until about a two-inch section is covered. Cut the yarn and tape it to the back of the plate. Start a new section of the yarn by repeating just what you did at first.

Keep wrapping the yarn and taping the ends to the back, overlapping the taped ends when you start a new section. Keep wrapping until the entire plate rim is covered, and it looks like a green wreath.

Use some red balls from the fringe or red pom-poms for the berries. Cut them off, and glue them on separately and in groups of three or four. Glue on a red bow at the top, and tie a piece of yarn onto the wreath and into a loop for hanging.

111. FIND YOUR PLACE!

 The plan: Everyone will know where to sit with these personalized place cards!

What it takes:

- Ruler
- Pencil
- Colored construction paper or 3"x 5" index cards
- Scissors
- Colored marking pens or crayons
- Old newspapers
- Stickers (optional)
- White glue (optional)
- Glitter (optional)

Use your ruler and pencil to measure and mark off three by five inches on the construction paper and cut it out with scissors, or use a ready-made index card. Fold the paper or card in half the long way. Lightly print a person's name on one side of the paper in your very best writing and go over it with a dark-colored marking pen. Have a grand time decorating the place card to go with the person or the season or even a special holiday.

Sports designs, dinosaurs, leaves for fall, and Christmas holly would all be eye-catchers, and stickers and glitter will really add some extra pizazz. Place a bit of glue here and there on your card, and when it's almost dry, put the card on a piece of newspaper and sprinkle some glitter onto the glue (the newspaper will catch any leftover sparkles). Now all you need to do is stand the place card up on the table just above where the plate is set, and everyone will know exactly where to sit!

112. CORNSTARCH MODELING CLAY

 The plan: Mix up a bowlful of modeling clay using cornstarch, oil, and flour!

What it takes:
- Large mixing bowl
- 1 cup cornstarch
- ⅓ cup vegetable oil
- Spoon
- ⅔ cup flour
- Large bowl
- Plastic wrap

Put the cornstarch in a bowl, and add the oil. Stir it with a spoon until it's smooth and looks like syrup. Add the flour, a little at a time, until the mixture is thick and getting hard to stir. Now use your hands to knead and squeeze the dough until it's smooth and feels like clay. If it doesn't feel stiff or hard enough to model, add a little more flour. You can use it right now to model all kinds of objects, or you can cover it with plastic wrap and store it in the refrigerator until you feel like being creative.

113. STRAW PAINTING

 The plan: Use a drinking straw to "blow" a painting into a kaleidoscope of colors!

What it takes:
- White butcher paper, shelf paper, or other slick paper
- Old newspapers
- Tempera paint
- Drinking straw
- Black fine-tip marking pen

Place the white paper on old newspapers on a table. Pour a small amount of the different colors of paint onto the paper in different areas. Put a straw in your mouth, and point the other end at an area of paint. Blow gently through the straw, pointing the straw in the direction you want the paint to go. When you blow through the straw the paint will fan out in different directions.

You can make some beautiful patterns when you cross one color over another. Try turning your paper around to get a different angle. When your picture is colorful and dry, use a fine-tip marking pen to turn it into a picture of specific things. You may also like it just the way it is without using a pen.

114. SNACK SACK

The plan: Make a crunchy trail mix treat.
What it takes:
- ¾ cup honey roasted peanuts
- 1½ cups honey graham cereal
- 1½ cups Cheerio-type cereal
- ½ cup raisins
- Gallon-size reclosable plastic bag

Wash your hands with soap and water. Then get out all of *What it takes.* Put peanuts, graham cereal, Cheerio-type cereal, and raisins into a reclosable plastic bag. Zip up the bag and shake it. Your Snack Sack is all ready for tasting. There will be plenty to share with your family, too.

115. PRETTY AS A PICTURE

The plan: Add beauty to an old picture frame by decorating it with buttons!
What it takes:
- Old glass-covered picture frame
- Old decorative buttons
- White glue

Look at the old picture frame. Decide where you could place buttons to make it more attractive. Set a few buttons of different colors and sizes in one corner of the frame to see how it looks. Move the buttons all around the picture frame to see where they look best. Keep the center of the glass free so a picture can be seen. Be creative with the colors, sizes, and shapes of the buttons.

When you have decided on the most eye-catching button arrangement, glue the buttons on with white glue. Let the glue dry thoroughly before putting a picture in the frame.

116. WATERING JUG

 The plan: Decorate a plastic watering can made from a milk jug!

What it takes:
- Plastic milk jug
- Pencil
- Scraps of colored contact paper
- Scissors

A plain plastic milk jug makes a wonderful watering can, but it would look a lot prettier if it were decorated with flowers, leaves, or some fancy design. Take a pencil and draw flower shapes or other designs from scraps of colored contact paper. Cut out your designs. Peel off the backing from the contact paper, and press the shapes onto the plastic jug. Now your Watering Jug will be a beauty to hold!

117. MAKE-A-JOURNAL

 The plan: Decorate a binder or other notebook that can be used as a personal journal!

What it takes:
- Old magazines
- Scissors
- Binder or other notebook
- White glue
- Photograph of you
- Black permanent marking pen

Look through old magazines. Cut out colorful pictures of activities you especially like. Is it football, fashions, or food? Arrange the cutouts on the cover of the binder or notebook. When the cutouts look just right, glue them down.

Glue your photograph right in the middle of the cover. Neatly write the word *Journal* somewhere on the cover. Now you must remember to write in your journal once or twice a week so you can remember all the exciting things you do.

118. MIRROR-RORRIM

 The plan: Draw what you see, without seeing what you draw!
What it takes:
- Plain white paper
- 3 to 4 books
- Hand mirror
- Pencil or pen

Sit down at a table and place a piece of paper in front of you. Place the pile of books behind the paper, and lean the mirror against the books so that it's standing up directly behind the paper.

Start this activity by writing or printing your name on the paper. Now look into the mirror and use your pencil or pen to trace over the letters of your name on the paper. Remember, don't peek at your paper; use only the mirror as your guide. This is harder than it seems!

Once you get the hang of it, and need a greater challenge, draw a picture while looking into the mirror, not at the paper. Try creating something simple at first, like a flower or a bird, before attempting to draw the Statue of Liberty!

For the *super* mirror artists, here's a *super* challenge: Look into the mirror and write your name or a word that looks correct in the mirror, then check to see how it came out on your paper. *Don't* peek at the paper while you're writing, wait until you've finished. How's that for a challenge? If you do it right, you may consider becoming a dentist when you grow up. Dentists work on your teeth by looking in a mirror some of the time.

119. EGG CARTON CREATURES

The plan: Stack several egg carton cups together to make animals or people!

What it takes:
- Cardboard egg carton
- Scissors
- White glue
- Tempera paint
- Paintbrushes
- Small Styrofoam ball
- Scraps of cloth, paper, yarn

Cut the egg carton into separate cups. Glue three stacked cups together. Decide what kind of creature you want to make. Maybe a ghost or maybe a bear. Paint the stacked cups white if you decide on a ghost, or brown if you want a bear. Glue on a small Styrofoam ball for a head. Paint on a face. Cut pieces of egg carton for ears or legs. Make clothing or hair from scraps of cloth and yarn, and glue in place. You can design all kinds of Egg Carton Creatures!

120. TIRE-TRACK WRAP

The plan: Make tire-track designer wrapping paper!

What it takes:
- Old newspapers
- 3 colors of poster paints
- 3 pie tins
- 9" x 12" piece of shelf paper or butcher paper
- 3 toy cars or trucks with wheels of varying sizes

Cover your work area with old newspaper. Select three colors of poster paint and pour each color into individual pie tins. Use just enough paint to cover the bottom of each pan.

Spread the 9" x 12" shelf paper or butcher paper on the work area. Dip the wheels of one toy in one color of paint and roll the toy over the shelf paper making any design you wish. Repeat with the other toys and colors until your design is brightly tire-tracked and beautiful. Let it dry.

While the wrapping paper is drying, clean up your work area and wash the cars and pie tins. Next time you have to wrap a gift, you have some very special wrapping paper!

121. PAINTED WAFERS

The plan: Decorate vanilla wafers "by painting" them with frosting.

What it takes:
- 1 can white frosting mix
- 5 small bowls
- Spoons
- Food coloring
- Vanilla wafers
- 1" clean paintbrush
- Small clean paintbrush
- Cup of water for rinsing
- Plate

Wash your hands with soap and water and get out all of *What it takes.* Place a large spoonful of white frosting mix in each bowl. Add a drop or two of food coloring into each bowl and stir. Wash the spoon before stirring another color. You can mix two colors to make a new color. For example, one drop of green plus five drops of blue make turquoise. Look on the food coloring box for mixing other colors.

Use a clean paintbrush to decorate the vanilla wafers. You can coat the whole wafer in one solid color with a couple of strokes of the one-inch paintbrush. You may want to make a face or a flower with the small brush. Wash the brushes before changing colors. Place each decorated wafer on a plate for sharing with family or friends.

122. CASSETTE CLUE

The plan: Record many different sounds on a tape recorder!

What it takes:
- Portable tape recorder
- Blank cassette tape
- Pencil
- Paper

What marvelous sounds do you hear around your house every day? Dripping water, wind in the trees, birds chirping, people talking, a baby crying, music playing? All of those noises are wonderful sounds for you to record.

Before starting, make certain the tape recorder batteries are working. Stop for a minute, and listen to the sounds inside your house. Decide which sound you want to record first, and go to where you are the closest to that sound. Before recording, write #1 on your paper with a pencil, and write exactly what sound you are recording. Press the record button and say, "This is sound number one." Let the tape record the sound for about thirty seconds before pushing the stop button. Now select another sound to record. Keep your paper and pencil handy for keeping track of the sounds and don't forget to speak the number before you record.

When you're finished you have a great sound guessing game to play with your family and friends.

123. WHAT'S FOR DINNER?

 The plan: Create a make-believe menu for dinner!
What it takes:
- Picture cookbook
- Pencil
- Piece of paper

The time for this activity is just before dinner, because that's when food sounds extra good. Get out a cookbook with lots of pretty food pictures. This puts you in the mood.

Pretend you are at a very fancy restaurant and can order anything you want for dinner. You'll have to select an *appetizer, soup, salad, main course* (including potato and vegetable), *drink,* and *dessert.* Is it making you hungry just thinking about it?

At the top of your paper, write "Menu." On the first line write "Appetizer." List your favorite one. Look in the cookbook if you can't think of one. On the second line, write "Soup." List a soup that you really like. On the third line, write "Salad." Choose a salad from the cookbook, or write the name of one of your favorites. You've got the idea now. Write "Main Course," "Drink," and "Dessert" and choose one of each.

By the time you finish this activity you'll rush to the kitchen yelling, "What's for dinner?"

124. DESIGNING WITH A COMB

The plan: Make beautiful designs by painting with a comb!

What it takes:
- Old newspaper
- White construction paper
- Comb
- Tempera paints
- Water

Cover your work area with old newspaper. Place your white construction paper in front of you. Now dip the comb into the tempera. Drag the comb across the paper any way you wish. Try some swirly flowers and clouds. You'll have to dip the comb into the paint each time you pick it up, but remember to rinse the comb under a water faucet before changing colors. Comb away!

125. FRUIT 'N' CONE

The plan: Fill an ice-cream cone with fruit!

What it takes:
- ½ cup strawberries
- Table knife
- Measuring cups
- 1 banana
- Small mixing bowl
- Mixing spoon
- 1 ice-cream cone
- 1 tablespoon honey
- 1 tablespoon granola (if you like it)

Thoroughly wash your hands with soap and water. Get out all of *What it takes*. Rinse the strawberries, and pull off the stems and green leaves. With a table knife slice the strawberries into a ½-cup measuring cup. Peel the banana and slice it into a ¼-cup measuring cup. Place all the sliced fruit into a mixing bowl and gently stir with a spoon.

Now scoop all the fruit into an ice-cream cone. Drizzle one tablespoon of honey over the fruit and top with a tablespoon of granola, if you like it. Your Fruit 'n' Cone is ready to eat when the kitchen is clean.

126. FAST GETAWAY

 The plan: Draw a floor plan of your home showing all exits to use in case of an emergency!

What it takes:
- Plain white paper
- Pencil with eraser
- Ruler
- Red marker
- Black fine-tip marking pen

If there was an emergency at your house and you and your family had to get out very quickly, how would you do it? Think about it. It is important to have a fast getaway plan and that all family members know about it. You can help by drawing a floor plan of your house showing the best ways to escape from each room.

At the top of a piece of paper write "Emergency Exits." Think of how your house would look if the roof was off, and you could look down from a helicopter. This will help you draw the floor plan of your house. Use a pencil and draw each floor of your house separately. Remember to write "door" and "window" in all the correct places.

Now draw arrows ⟶ in red to point to the places in each room that would make the best escape routes (exits). Windows and doors are exits. Try to find *two ways* to get out of each room if you can.

Now that your floor plan and exit arrows are in place, go over all the lines of your floor plan with the black fine-tip marking pen, and write the names inside each room like "kitchen" and "bedroom."

Now that you've made your plan, check with your parents or guardian to see if it follows proper safety rules.

127. MUFFIN TIN ROLL

 The plan: Test your skill by rolling a small ball up a cardboard ramp into muffin tin cups!

What it takes:
- Muffin tin
- Cardboard as big as the muffin tin
- Pencil
- Scissors
- Masking tape
- Sugarless candy or other small treats—one for each muffin cup
- Small ball

Place the muffin tin on the piece of cardboard. Trace around the muffin tin with a pencil and then cut the cardboard the same size as the muffin tin. Tape the cardboard piece to the long side of the muffin tin so that it hangs off the side like a ramp. Place a piece of sugarless candy or small treat into each muffin cup.

Take five steps back from the cardboard ramp, and roll a small ball toward the muffin tin. When it goes up the ramp and into a cup, the goodie is yours.

128. CAMPING ON PAPER

 The plan: Find pictures of camping equipment you need for a week in the woods!

What it takes:
- Old catalogs and magazines
- Scissors
- White drawing paper
- Black fine-tip marking pen
- Glue stick

Pretend you and your friends are going on a camping trip for one whole week, and you have to collect all the equipment. What would you take?

Look through old catalogs and magazines, and cut out pictures of camping equipment such as a tent, sleeping bags, lantern, something to cook on, and maybe even a fishing pole. You might even find pictures of food and a truck to carry all the equipment.

On the top piece of drawing paper, write "Camping Trip" with a fine-tip marking pen. Arrange all the camping equipment pictures on the paper, and glue them down. Wouldn't it be fun to make this paper dream come true?

129. PIPE CLEANER PERSON

 The plan: Create a doll by twisting pipe cleaners and attaching a round cork head!

What it takes:

- 1 large bead
- 3 pipe cleaners
- Black marking pen
- Scraps of crepe paper
- Scissors
- Yarn scraps
- White glue
- Small piece of cardboard

Push one end of a pipe cleaner through the hole in the bead. Bend the end of the pipe cleaner so the bead won't come out. Form two arms by taking another pipe cleaner and twisting it around the center of the first pipe cleaner under the bead head to make a "T" shape. These arms will stick straight out. Twist the last pipe cleaner around and down the body beginning under the head to form a leg. The first pipe cleaner with the bead attached is another leg. Bend the ends of both legs to form feet.

Draw a face on the bead with a permanent black marking pen. Cut and glue pieces of crepe paper for clothes. Make hair by gluing scraps of yarn to the head. If you want your Pipe Cleaner Person to stand up, glue the feet to a small piece of cardboard.

130. DOT · DOT · DASH—

 The plan: Learn how to send a flashlight message in Morse code.

What it takes:
- Flashlight
- Morse code signals

More than 100 years ago Robert Morse invented a *dot-dot-dash* alphabet system called the Morse code. This dot-and-dash alphabet was used to send telegrams over telegraph wires. Sailors sent the dots and dashes with big lights to signal other ships at sea. Today, campers lost in the woods might use flashlight signals to say "Help!"

Look at the International Morse code below. With your flashlight, practice each letter. Dots are made by flashing the light off and on very fast. For dashes, leave the light on a little longer. The international signal for help is S-O-S. Can you signal an S-O-S?

A	• —	N	— •
B	— • • •	O	— — —
C	— • — •	P	• — — •
D	— • •	Q	— — • —
E	•	R	• — •
F	• • — •	S	• • •
G	— — •	T	—
H	• • • •	U	• • —
I	• •	V	• • • —
J	• — — —	W	• — —
K	— • —	X	— • • —
L	• — • •	Y	— • — —
M	— —	Z	— — • •

Practice flashing your name in code. The "help" signal is used most often, so be sure you practice flashing it. When you think you've got it, try to send your signal in a dark room.

131. FEED THE BIRDS

The plan: String popcorn on dental floss as a tasty treat for birds!

What it takes:

- Large-eye needle
- 8 feet of dental floss
- Scissors
- Popped popcorn

It is a cinch to make the birds in your neighborhood sing with joy when you invite them to a popcorn feed. Thread a needle with eight feet of dental floss, pull the floss through the needle, and tie the two ends together.

String the popcorn onto the dental floss by pushing the needle through a piece of popcorn and sliding it toward the end with the knot. When the floss is nearly filled with popcorn, cut the needle from the floss. Tie the cut ends together.

Go outside, and tie your popcorn string between two bushes or trees. In no time at all, the word will get out, and you'll have some new fine-feathered friends.

132. SURPRISE GREETING

The plan: Fold a dime in layers of paper, seal it in an envelope, and send it to a friend!

What it takes:

- 6 pieces of lined paper
- Scissors
- 1 dime or other coin
- White glue
- Pencil
- Envelope

Cut the lined papers into six squares, each one a different size. Stack the papers according to size with the largest paper on the bottom of the pile. Glue a dime or other coin to the middle of the smallest paper, and fold it so the dime cannot be seen. Write, "Here it is!" on the outside of the folded paper. Fold the next square of paper and write another little message like, "You're nearly there!" Continue folding the papers one at a time until all six papers are folded and messages written on each one. Try to keep the folds as flat as you can.

Write a person's name on the envelope and put your surprise greeting *inside*. What a treat when your friend or family member finds the little treasure!

133. RUBBER BALL SLALOM

 The plan: Create an obstacle course for bikes, trikes, roller skates, or in-line skates!

What it takes:
- 8 small pieces of paper
- Black marking pen
- 8 rubber balls
- Transparent tape
- Bicycle, tricycle, roller skates, or in-line skates

Number the eight small pieces of paper with a black marking pen from one through eight. Tape a number to each rubber ball with the transparent tape. Outside, in a very open area, place the balls so you can ride or skate around them.

Select a starting point near the ball marked number one. Ride or skate around the obstacle course without hitting any of the marked balls. You must follow the numbers in order. If you touch a ball or miss a number, you have to begin again. Don't worry if the balls move around. This just makes the slalom more fun.

To test your slalom skills, make the course more difficult by placing the balls closer together.

134. PEBBLE NAMEPLATE

 The plan: Make a nameplate for your desk using tiny rocks glued to poster board!

What it takes:
- Small pebbles
- Mixing bowl
- Water
- Towel
- 6" x 12" poster board
- Black marking pen
- White glue

Collect a large handful of very little rocks (pebbles). In a mixing bowl filled with water, thoroughly clean the pebbles. Dry them on a towel.

Fold the 6" x 12" piece of poster board in half the long way. With the fold at the top, print your name in the middle of the top section with a pencil. Keep the letters evenly spaced. Open the poster board so that it's lying flat. Carefully squeeze a line of white glue on the first letter of your name. Place pebbles along the line of glue. Glue and place pebbles one letter at a time on all the letters until your nameplate is finished.

When the glue dries, fold the poster board again, and you have a permanent pebble nameplate for your desk.

135. IT'S ALL WET

 The plan: Dip paper in water and create a work of art with chalk.

What it takes:
- Old newspapers
- White construction paper
- Large bowl
- Water
- Colored chalk
- Scissors

Cover your work area with newspapers. Now dip a piece of white construction paper into a bowl of water. Hold the paper over the bowl, and let the extra water drip off. Now lay the wet paper onto the newspaper, and draw a picture on the wet paper with the chalk. Your picture will be bold and bright! Let the paper dry before moving it. If by chance your picture sticks to the newspaper, don't worry. Just trim off the newspaper with your scissors and have a black-and-white backing for your beautiful creation.

136. FLOATING PARACHUTE

The plan: Make a handkerchief parachute!

What it takes:

- Ball of string
- Ruler
- Scissors
- Square handkerchief
- Medium-sized rock
- Transparent tape

Measure and cut four pieces of string twelve inches long. Spread out the handkerchief and tie one piece of string to each corner. Wrap each of the four loose string ends around your rock two times. Tape the wrapped strings to the rock to make sure they will not come loose. Your parachute is now ready to launch.

Go outside, and wrap the parachute around the rock. Now throw it up as high as you can, and watch it float to the ground. Make sure you're not standing under it when it comes down!

137. QUICKIE HAND PUPPET

The plan: Create a simple puppet by folding a piece of paper and adding facial features!

What it takes:

- Piece of plain white paper
- Transparent tape
- Scraps of colored construction paper
- Pencil
- Scissors
- Glue

Fold the plain white paper in three parts from the bottom to the top the long way. Tape the loose edge down. Now fold the paper in half the short way. Make two "wings" by folding each end in half again to meet the fold. When you hold the middle fold it will kind of look like a paper airplane.

Try putting four fingers into one open end of the paper and your thumb into the other open end. Move your fingers and thumb out and in a few times. Doesn't it look like a wide mouth? Use your imagination! With a pencil draw some big teeth on scraps of colored construction paper. Draw funny eyes, ears, nose, and maybe a tongue, too. Cut these pieces out, and glue them onto your hand puppet.

138. TV FOR ME

 The plan: Choose the TV programs you would like to watch during the week!

What it takes:
- Piece of lined paper
- Pencil
- Weekly TV listing from the newspaper or the *TV Guide*

Use your pencil to write the days of the week across the top of your paper. Leave space for listing times, TV shows, and channel numbers under each day.

Find the weekly TV guide from the newspaper. It is usually in the Sunday section, or use the *TV Guide* magazine if you have it. Look through the listings for each day. Write the time, channel number, and name of the shows you want to see.

Better show your personal TV guide to your parents before making too many TV plans!

139. TOSS-AND-REACH HOPSCOTCH

 The plan: Draw a nine-square hopscotch and learn how to play!
What it takes:
- Chalk
- Small beanbag, flat rock, or a large eraser for a marker

Find a large smooth area of cement, and with the chalk draw nine squares that are larger than your foot. Make three rows with three squares in each row. Leave about one foot of space between each square. When all the squares are drawn, give each box a number except the middle square. Start #1 on the bottom right square with #2 just above #1. Finish numbering in a counterclockwise direction, ending with #8 right next to #1. Leave the middle square blank.

You are ready to play Toss-and-Reach Hopscotch, but first you must know three basic rules for all hopscotch games. First, your feet, hands, or the marker may never touch a chalk line. If the marker or your feet touch a line, you must begin again. Second, if you lose your balance and fall you must start again. Third, you always hop on one foot.

To begin the game, toss your marker into the middle square with no number. Hop into square #1, lean over without losing your balance or touching any lines, pick up the marker, and hop back out. Toss the marker into the middle again, hop into square #1 and then into #2. Pick up the marker and hop back out through #1. Repeat this procedure until you reach #8. You must hop only on one foot. When you've perfected hopping on the right foot, try doing it on the left.

140. SIMPLE YARN DOLL

The plan: Make a simple yarn doll!

What it takes:
- Scissors
- Ruler
- 8" x 3" piece of cardboard
- Ball of old yarn

Cut off six pieces of yarn about as long as the piece of cardboard. These pieces will be "tying pieces." Set these aside.

Now take the ball of yarn, and wrap it around the eight-inch piece of cardboard many, many times, going the long way. When the yarn feels very thick, cut the yarn at one end of the cardboard, one or two strands at a time. Lay the cardboard down, and gently lift it from one side, keeping the yarn flat and all together.

Take a tying piece you have set aside, and slip it under the pile of yarn near the top, where a neck might be. Tie the ends tightly. Above the tie will be the head of the doll. Now divide off yarn strands from each side of the yarn for two arms. Trim the arm strands with the scissors so the arms are not too long. Slip a tying piece where the doll's wrists would be and tie firmly. Leave hands of yarn beneath the tie to make the wrists.

Find a spot on the yarn doll's body where its waist should be, and tie it off with a tying piece. Next, divide the yarn into two legs, and with tying pieces tie off the doll's ankles, leaving yarn feet at the ends. By using larger pieces of cardboard you can make even bigger yarn dolls!

141. HELPFUL NUMBERS

 The plan: Collect emergency telephone numbers and place them near the phone!

What it takes:
- 5" x 7" card
- Pen
- Telephone book

There are many telephone numbers you and your family use every day. You probably have those memorized. There are some phone numbers you need to find quickly, but you do not use every day. Some of those numbers include the Fire Station closest to your home, the Police Department nearest your home, your Doctor's Office, and your School Office.

On a 5" x 7" card list these places with a pen. Look in the telephone book for the correct phone numbers, and write the number clearly next to the place. You may think of some other very important places to add to the list, such as neighbors or others you can call if you have a problem. The number 911 is the best number to know, but only call it in case of an emergency or life-threatening situation.

When the telephone numbers are written clearly on the card, place the card near the telephone. Everyone in the family will thank you for the help.

142. ITSY-BITSY FLOWERPOTS

 The plan: Make sponge flowers to plant in flowerpots made from old toothpaste lids!

What it takes:

- Colored sponge
- Scissors
- Pencil
- Green pipe cleaner
- Ruler
- Scraps of green construction paper
- White glue
- 2 old toothpaste lids
- Modeling clay

Cut four tiny flower shapes from the colored sponge. Draw them first if you have to. Cut four three-inch pieces of green pipe cleaner. These are your stems. Push a pipe cleaner "stem" into each flower shape. Cut small leaves from green construction paper scraps, and glue them onto the stems.

Fill two old toothpaste lids with modeling clay, and plant the pipe cleaner stems by sticking them deep into the clay, two flowers for each Itsy-Bitsy Flowerpot. Your flowers will brighten anyone's day!

143. CHOCOLATE THUMBPRINTS

 The plan: Mix up a batch of no-bake chocolate cookies that melt in your mouth!

What it takes:

- ¼ cup soft butter (½ stick)
- Mixing bowl
- Small tray
- Waxed paper
- Pie tin
- Chocolate sprinkles
- Measuring spoons
- 6 tablespoons cocoa powder
- 3 tablespoons powdered sugar

Take the butter out of the refrigerator and put it in a mixing bowl twenty-five minutes before you start so the butter becomes soft.

First, wash your hands with soap and water. Then get out all of *What it takes.* Cover the small tray with waxed paper, and pour chocolate sprinkles into a pie tin. Measure the cocoa powder and powdered sugar into the mixing bowl, and with clean hands combine with the soft butter until it is all blended together. This is your dough.

Knead the dough with your hands until it feels very smooth. Shape the dough into small balls with your fingers, and roll each ball in the chocolate sprinkles. Place the sprinkled chocolate balls on the wax-papered tray. Put your thumbprint gently in the middle of each round ball. Store the chocolate thumbprints in the refrigerator. Don't lick your thumb until all the chocolate balls are thumbprinted!

144. PLATE FACES

 The plan: Make a face mask from a paper plate!
What it takes:

- Paper plate
- Colored marking pens or crayons
- Scissors
- Hole punch
- 2 12" pieces of string

With colored marking pens or crayons draw a funny, scary, or fancy face on a paper plate. Cut out the center of the eyes that are drawn on the plate. Punch two holes about an inch from the edge of the plate, even with the eyes, but a little higher. Now cut two pieces of string about as long as your head. Tie a string through each punched hole, and make a knot. Now place the plate in front of your face, tie the strings together behind your head, and get ready to make everyone laugh.

145. COLOR DROP AND SWIVEL

 The plan: Swirl liquid tempera paint onto a paper plate and form beautiful patterns!
What it takes:

- Old newspapers
- Spoons (one for each color)
- Liquid tempera paint
- Paper plate

Cover your work area with old newspapers. Place a spoon in each jar of liquid tempera paint. Drop small spoonfuls of paint from several colors onto a paper plate. Swivel (turn) the plate slowly back and forth to create a colorful design. It takes many twists and turns for a design to form, so be patient. Look at the new colors and beautiful shapes you can make! Let the plate dry, and it will turn into a work of modern art!

146. FLOWER PRINTS

 The plan: Use fresh flowers to paint lovely designs!

What it takes:
- Fresh flowers (dandelions are great)
- Old newspapers
- 3 colors of liquid tempera
- 3 pie tins or paper plates
- Plain white paper

First, go outside, and pick a few fresh flowers or weeds, at least three, one for each color paint. Dandelions will work fine. Now cover your work area with old newspaper. Then pour three different colors of tempera into separate pie tins or paper plates. Place a piece of white paper in front of you.

Gently dip a flower into one color, and *lightly* touch the flower onto the piece of paper several times. Use a different flower for each color. If you have two different kinds of flowers, try dipping another flower for a different design. What special effects you can make with flowers and weeds!

147. ROY G. BIV

 The plan: Find out that making a rainbow is as simple as re-membering this name!

What it takes:
- Colored marking pens or crayons
- Plain white paper
- Pencil

Have you ever seen a rainbow? There is nothing more beautiful than the colors that magically appear after a rainstorm. The colors of the rainbow are always the same, even if the rainbow is on another continent. A rainbow in Africa has the same colors as a rainbow in Australia or America, and the colors are always in the same order. The colors of the rainbow are:

Red **O**range **Y**ellow   **G**reen   **B**lue **I**ndigo **V**iolet

Do you see what the first letters spell out? *Roy G. Biv!* This is the exact order of a rainbow from top to bottom. Is there a color that you're not sure about? If it's indigo, this is a color between violet and blue. If you don't have a blue-violet crayon or marker, simply combine blue and violet. You may already know that violet is another name for purple.

Take your pencil and sketch an outline of a rainbow on your plain white paper, and make it as large or small as you would like. Then, use your colored marking pens or crayons to color it in. Remember that red goes on top and violet goes on the bottom. Now you can create a rainbow anywhere, anytime, as long as you remember the name *Roy G. Biv!!*

148. PAPER TOWEL WRAP-UP

 The plan: Create wrapping paper by squirting tempera paint onto damp paper towels!

What it takes:
- Old newspapers
- Liquid tempera paint (4 or 5 colors)
- Small bowls for each color
- Water
- Paper towels
- Eyedropper

Cover your work area with old newspapers. Pour a little tempera paint into each bowl. Make the paint thin by adding a little water to each bowl. Get three or four sections of paper towel damp by sprinkling them with water.

Spread one paper towel section at a time on dry newspaper. Use the eyedropper to squirt different colors of paint onto the damp paper towel. Rinse the eyedropper each time you change colors. The colors will run together to make beautiful shapes and designs. Paint several paper towels for great wrapping paper, but be sure the paper is dry before wrapping a present!

149. A FLOWERY GREETING

 The plan: Create a greeting card using dried flowers!

What it takes:

- White construction paper
- Small dried or fresh flowers
- White glue
- Clear contact paper
- Scissors

Fold the construction paper in half. You can fold it in either direction. Select one or more dried or fresh flowers. Arrange the flowers on the front half of the card. When it looks just right, glue the flowers to the card. Let it dry.

Open the card, lay it flat, and place clear contact paper over the front and back of the card. Do this very gently or the flower will break. Trim off any excess contact paper. Fold it again, and now your card can be put away until you are ready to give it to someone on a special day!

150. WATER BOTTLE WEIGHTS

 The plan: Use empty plastic bottles to fill and help make muscles!

What it takes:

- 2 empty quart plastic water bottles with lids
- Old newspapers
- Spoon
- Sand or fine dirt
- Water

You don't need expensive weights to build muscles. All you need are two empty plastic water bottles with lids.

Here's what you do: Spread some newspapers on the ground outside and then use a spoon to fill the bottles with sand or fine dirt. If you don't have sand or dirt, the "weights" will work just fine filled with water. Put the lids on the bottles, and you're ready to build those muscles.

Hold a bottle in each hand and bend your elbows, bringing the weights to your chest. Repeat ten times. Another exercise you can do is to push the weights above your head. Still another exercise is to bend

SUPER FUN FOR ONE

your knees and squat down while holding a weight in each hand.
Move over, Arnold S.!

151. MOVE TO THE MUSIC

 The plan: Play beautiful music and create a work of art!

What it takes:
- Colored marking pens or crayons
- Large piece of butcher paper
- Music from a tape, CD, or radio

Get out your colored marking pens or crayons, and spread a large piece of paper in front of you on a table. Turn on your favorite music and let the sound and rhythm tell you how to color. You could put a color in each hand. Let your arms and hands move to the beat. Change colors whenever you want. Your imagination can make beautiful designs right in time with the music.

152. CELERY SNACKS

 The plan: Fill celery stalks with a favorite filling and enjoy!

What it takes:
- Washed celery stalks (as many as you want to eat)
- Paper towel
- Spoon
- Peanut butter, cream cheese, or cottage cheese
- Raisins, chocolate chips, pineapple bits, apple pieces, or other fruit bits

Wash your hands with soap and water, and then get out all of *What it takes*. Dry each piece of celery with a paper towel so the filling you put in will stay put. Use a spoon to spread your favorite filling along the celery groove. After the filling is in place, decorate the filling with raisins, chocolate chips, or fruit bits. Crunchy celery is very tasty with all that good stuff inside, and maybe you'll come up with a special stuffing of your own!

153. BOOK HOP AND JUMP

 The plan: Hop and jump over a book obstacle course!

What it takes:
• 7 or 8 hardcover books

Here's a good game for building leg muscles. With the permission of your parents, collect seven or eight hardcover books and lay them on the floor in a straight line about two feet apart. Now stand at the end of your book line and with both feet jump over each book in the line. That's pretty easy, so now try hopping over the line of books on your right foot, and then go back up the book line hopping on your left foot. When you've hopped up and down a few times, try standing the books up straight. See if you can first jump over them with both feet, and then hop up and down the book line without knocking any down.

When you want a change in your hopping and jumping, stand the books three feet apart in a circle. See how many times you can hop and jump around the circle without knocking the books down. You'll be ready for a rest after all this exercise!

154. GREEN GARDEN GROWING

 The plan: Create your own garden by planting vegetable tops!

What it takes:
• 1 old shallow baking pan
• Sand enough to cover ½" on the pan bottom
• Garden soil to cover 1" on the bottom of the pan
• Top half inch of 5 or 6 fresh carrots
• Top half inch of 3 fresh radishes, turnips, or beets (optional)
• Jar of water

This garden will look like a jungle once it begins to grow. Cover the bottom of your shallow baking pan with a one-half-inch layer of sand. Now cover the sand with one inch of garden soil. Get your little vegetable tops and plant them in the soil at least three inches apart. Let the top of each vegetable show above the soil. Water your garden thoroughly, and then place the pan in a well-lighted area. Water your garden a little each day and soon sprouts will appear. If you are patient, it won't be long until you will have a whole green garden growing.

155. BLEACH BOTTLE BIRD FEEDER

 The plan: Make a bird feeder from a plastic bleach bottle!
What it takes:
- 1-gallon plastic bleach bottle
- Pencil
- Scissors
- 18" thin wire or piece of rope
- Birdseed

Draw a large "window" shape with a pencil on one side of the plastic bottle. It can be a square shape or a rectangle, or even an egg shape. Make it large enough so that the bottom of the window is about two inches up from the bottom of the bottle and about one inch under the handle at the top. This will be the window or door for the birds that will visit your feeder. Cut out this section by poking a hole in the center of the window with your scissors and then cutting around your pencil line.

Thread a piece of wire or rope through the handle of the bottle to attach the bird feeder to a low, thick tree branch. The trunk of the tree will help balance the bottle. Sprinkle birdseed in the bottom of the bottle, and when you're out of sight, wait very quietly for the birds to arrive!

156. STRICTLY FOR THE BIRDS!

 The plan: Stale bread slices cut with a cookie cutter are just what the birdies love!

What it takes:
- Cookie cutters
- Several slices of stale bread
- Paper towel
- Bent paper clip
- Yarn or string
- Spatula
- Peanut butter
- Birdseed (optional)

First you must find a tree you would like to use for your bird feeder.

Use a cookie cutter to cut shapes out of bread slices on a paper towel. Take a bent paper clip, and poke a hole about an inch from the top of your bread shape. Thread a piece of yarn or string through the hole, and tie a knot near the bread. Leave some extra yarn to tie your bread shape to the tree. Next, use a spatula to spread each cutout with peanut butter. If you have any birdseed, the birds would love some sprinkled on the peanut butter.

Hang your cookie cutter bird treat on a tree branch, and if you can't reach high enough, wait until an adult can help you. Caution: Keep your feeder out of reach of animals of the whiskered and purring kind!

THIRTY-MINUTE ACTIVITIES

Your homework is finished. You've walked the dog. Mom's cooking. Dad's reading the newspaper. You're as restless as a bug on a toad's tongue (eek!), and you've got **Thirty Minutes** until dinner! You've already frozen those **Paintsicles** so get ready to make a very cool picture. What's a **Paintsicle**? Read on!

157. DON'T LICK THESE "PAINTSICLES!"

 The plan: You'll have a real cool picture when you paint with these frozen "paintsicles!"

What it takes:
- Plastic popsicle molds or ice cube trays
- Tempera paint
- Popsicle sticks or tongue depressors
- White paper, butcher paper, or shelf paper works well for big pictures

You can get ready for this activity anytime, and then do it a day or two later. Fill popsicle molds or ice cube trays with different colors of tempera paint. Freeze until thickened and then insert a popsicle stick in the center of each one. Freeze until firm.

When you're ready for your "cool" activity, loosen the "paintsicle" by jiggling the popsicle mold, or dip the bottom in some warm water for a few seconds. Use your "paintsicle" just like you would use a fat marking pen, and when you finish with each color be sure to put it right back in the mold and the freezer so it won't melt too quickly. Cool, huh?

158. OLYMPIC FLAG

 The plan: Design an Olympic flag for your hometown or city!

What it takes:
- White drawing paper
- Pencil
- Colored marking pens or crayons

Pretend that the Olympics are going to be held right in your own hometown or city, and that you've been asked to design the official flag for these games. Every Olympic Games has its own flag, complete with a logo, the name of the city, and the year of the event. The flags also display the five Olympic rings, consisting of three rings on top and two underneath. Have you seen these rings on the Olympic logo? Look in your encyclopedia or ask an adult if you haven't.

Get your drawing paper and a pencil ready, and create a logo or symbol for your flag. Now add the Olympic rings, the name of your town or city, and the year that the Games will be held. Make your flag eye-catching and colorful. After all, you want to attract as many spectators from all over the world as possible!

159. MORNING WAKE-UP CALL

 The plan: Invent a device guaranteed to wake up any sleepyhead!

What it takes
- Lined or plain paper
- Pencil
- Colored marking pens or crayons

Getting up in the morning can be a real chore for some people, but that could all change with your "wonder wake-up" invention. Think up a sure-fire gadget that will be safe yet certain to get even the sleepiest person out of bed in a flash. Maybe it will make noise, flash lights, or even smell!

Whatever you come up with, use a pencil to write a detailed description on a piece of paper, and of course, a true inventor will always make a detailed sketch. Color your invention in with marking pens or crayons. And the name of this wonder invention is _____?

160. A VERY SWEET STORY

The plan: Make up a super sweet tale using the names of candy to tell your story!

What it takes:
- Paper
- Pencil

The names of yummy, sweet candy treats can be used to develop the tastiest stories ever. Think of the names of your favorite candy bars like the chocolate, marshmallow, almond, toffee, caramel, peanut butter, taffy, and mint kind of sweet treats.

Next, use a pencil and paper to make a list of all the candy bars and goodies you can think of. Now take a look at the names. Think of a simple story you can write using as many names as you can. How about something like this, just for starters:

Now or Later you may **Snicker** about how the people **Look** who come from **Mars.** They came here by riding a **Tootsie Roll** through the **Milky Way,** of all things. What a funny sight! Of course, they had to hike up to the **Summit** where the **Three Musketeers** live before they reached the home of **Baby Ruth.** This adorable baby was one of the famous **Sugar Babies,** and the crazy men from **Mars** turned out to be **Lifesavers** when they rescued **Baby Ruth** from the **Whatchamacallit!**

There are **Good & Plenty** more candy bars and candy treats, and now it's up to you to create the sweetest story you've ever told!

161. TABLE SETTING PLACEMATS

The plan: You'll always know where to put the silverware when you make these placemats!

What it takes:
- 12"x 18" colored construction paper
- Silverware, glass, cup, and saucer
- Colored marking pens and crayons
- Dinner plate
- Pencil
- Clear contact paper

The guessing will be over when you make a set of these placemats for your family. Take a piece of construction paper and place a dinner plate in the center. Trace around it with your pencil. Next, place a table knife on the right hand side of the plate with the blade turned toward the plate. The spoon goes on the outside of the knife. The fork goes on the left side of the plate, and if you're using a salad fork, place it on the outside of the big fork. Now, all you have to do is use your pencil to trace around the silverware pieces. Place a glass above the knife and a saucer right next to it for the coffee cup. Trace around these. If you'd like to add a salad plate, you can put this above the fork. Trace around everything!

Use a dark marking pen to go over your pencil lines so they'll show up. Decorate your placemat with marking pens or crayons to look like a printed tablecloth or fabric placemat. Stripes, checks, flowers, and just about anything colorful will look terrific. Cover both sides with clear contact paper, leaving about one-half-inch overlap on all four sides. Trim the contact paper with your scissors, and you're ready to set any table perfectly the next time Mom or Dad needs some help!!

162. JUICY PUPPETS

 The plan: Make a puppet with a juice can and extra odds and ends!

What it takes:
- Empty frozen juice cans without the tops
- Tempera paint
- Paintbrush
- Construction paper
- Scissors
- Fabric scraps, buttons, sequins, ribbon, felt, cotton balls, fake fur, beads
- White glue

Paint a juice can with tempera paint, and let it dry. Tape the inside edge of the can so there are no sharp edges. Next, turn the can so that the open end is down, and then paint on eyes, eyebrows, lashes, a nose, mouth, and whiskers (if it's a cat) and maybe a mustache (if it's a man), or use cutouts of construction paper.

Use scissors to cut long strips of felt or fabric for the arms and legs. Glue the legs on the inside of the can opening so they hang down. Glue the arms onto the sides of the can. Glue a small button where the feet and hands should go so that they'll be weighted down.

You can add animal or people ears to the top of the can, and even some yarn or fake fur hair. To work the puppets, put your fingers in the can!

163. JACK-O'-LANTERN PARADE

 The plan: Use egg carton cups glued together to make a jack-o'-lantern parade!

What it takes:

- Empty egg carton
- Scissors
- White glue
- Orange tempera paint
- Paintbrush
- Black fine-tip marking pen or black construction paper

Cut out the cups from the egg carton. Take one of the cups. Now squeeze some glue around the edge of the part that you've cut, and place another cup on top, with the cut edges matching. This will be a fat pumpkin! Hold in place for a minute or two until it sticks. Do the same with other cups so that you will have two cups glued together to make more pumpkins. When the glue is dry, paint them with orange paint.

When the paint is dry, use a black marking pen to make eyes, nose, and mouth, or cut out black construction paper shapes and glue them on. Your jack-o'-lanterns will look great on a bookshelf, table, or windowsill.

164. BUBBLE UP!

 The plan: Make the biggest, weirdest, fattest bubbles on the block!

What it takes:

- 18" piece of thin wire that can easily be bent and shaped
- Shallow pans that the wire wands can be dipped into
- Liquid dish soap
- Water

Hold the piece of wire in your hand. About five inches up from the end that you're holding in your hand, bend the wire to make a simple shape such as a circle, oval, heart, square, or just a free-form shape. The five-inch piece that you're holding in your hand will be the handle. Now, carefully pour the liquid soap into a pan and add a little water if it's too thick. Go outside and try out your "bubble machine" by dipping the wand into the soap and lifting it out. Wave the wand slowly through the air, and watch the bubbles appear and float up, up, and away!

165. SHAKE AND GUESS

 The plan: Shake a die (one of a pair of dice) and *guess* what numbers will come up!

What it takes:
- Piece of paper
- Pencil
- 1 die (half of a pair of dice)

Across the top of a piece of paper write the numbers 1, 2, 3, 4, 5, 6, and draw a box under each number. You are going to shake and roll the die six times to play the game. Before you shake and roll the die, you decide how many times each of the six numbers will come up. Write the numbers you guess in each box.

If you think that the number 6 will come up two times in the six rolls, you would write the number 2 in the box under the 6. Clue: When you add the numbers in all six boxes, the total must equal six. Some of the boxes may have a 0 in them because you don't think that number will come up at all in six tries. After the first six rolls, change the numbers and roll again!

How many shakes and rolls of the die will it take you to match your guesses? Make sure you count!

six shakes	A miracle!
twelve shakes	Unbelievable!
eighteen shakes	Fantastic!
twenty-four shakes	Great!
thirty shakes +	This is not your lucky day!

166. COPY CAT

 The plan: Make your own carbon paper with this simple recipe!
What it takes:

- 2 or more pieces of white paper
- Crayons
- Ballpoint pen

Use as many deep-colored crayons as you'd like to color in one entire side of a piece of white paper. Use lots of different colors, but the darker shades work best. Next, place the crayon-colored paper *facedown* on top of the second piece of white paper. Now you're ready to draw a picture on the top piece of paper, which is the back of the one you've colored. Use a ballpoint pen and press down hard, because you want the colored side to transfer onto the blank page on the bottom.

You're now going to be in for a colorful surprise when you remove your "carbon paper" from the top and see that your drawing is now a rainbow of beautiful shades of blue and purple, green, red, and orange. What other colors will you choose next?

When you've finished be sure to save your colored "carbon paper" for another picture.

167. WINDOW TRACINGS

 The plan: Use a window with sunlight shining through to make great tracings!

What it takes:
- A window during the daytime
- Something you want to trace
- Masking or transparent tape
- Lightweight white paper such as copy-machine paper
- Pencil
- Black fine-tip marking pen
- Colored marking pens or crayons

Find a picture of something you'd like to trace. A drawing will work better than a photograph, and look for a picture that has dark lines so it will be easier to see. Hold the picture up to the window, and keep it in place with a tiny strip of tape on the top and bottom edges taped to the window. Place a plain piece of lightweight white paper over the picture, and also hold it in place with tiny strips of tape attached to the window.

Use your pencil to trace the picture. The light coming through the window will help you see what to trace. When you finish tracing you may like how it looks done in pencil, or you may want to go over your pencil lines with a fine-tip marking pen. You can even color in your tracing.

168. SIDEWALK CHALK TALK

 The plan: Make a marvelous mural on your sidewalk or driveway with washable chalk!

What it takes:
• Several colors of washable sidewalk chalk

Use a light-colored piece of chalk to sketch in your mural (large picture) on a sidewalk, driveway, game court, or other area of concrete. Think what would it be like to create your own super solar system with new planets, moons, stars, and maybe even a comet or two.

After everything is outlined, begin filling in areas by using the side of a piece of chalk. For some finishing touches try outlining objects with your darkest chalk color so they'll really stand out. Don't forget to ask permission first from Mom or Dad, and be sure to tell them that this chalk drawing will disappear in a flash with a few splashes of water. There are as many ideas for you to draw as there are colors of the rainbow, so whatever you do, think colorful and have fun being a sidewalk designer!

169. SILHOUETTE MURAL

 The plan: Using dark paper on light, you can make a stunning silhouette mural!

What it takes:
- Pencil
- Black or dark construction paper
- Scissors
- Piece of white construction paper or poster board
- White glue

Use your pencil to draw outline shapes of subjects on the black or dark construction paper. Carefully cut out the drawings and start arranging them on your white or light-colored construction paper or poster board to form a mural. Switch them around until they're in just the right place.

A landscape with trees, houses, flowers, clouds, hills, fences, and maybe an animal would make a beautiful silhouette mural, but so would a vase of flowers or a football player with his arm reaching back to throw a pass. Hockey players on the ice, a ballerina on her toes, or a mother duck with her babies following her would also make a stunning silhouette. Think black on white. Think simple lines, and all you have to do after getting the objects placed where you'd like is to glue them on!

170. A WATER SYMPHONY

 The plan: You'll be making music as soon as you fill up eight drinking glasses and strike them!

What it takes:
- 8 matching *glass* drinking glasses (not plastic)
- Water
- Metal or wooden spoon

You'll be conducting your own orchestra in no time when you line up eight matching drinking glasses in a row on the kitchen countertop. Now all you have to do is fill each glass with water, starting with the first glass on your left. Fill the first glass all the way to the top. As you go down the line of glasses, put a little less water in each glass, until glass #8 (the last one on your right) has just a tiny bit of water in it.

Now it's time to tune up the "orchestra" by striking each glass on its side with the spoon. If you know your Do-Re-Mi's, you can tune up by singing, "Do-Re-Me-Fa-So-La-Ti-Do."

Have you discovered that the glass with the most water has the lowest sound, and the glass with the tiny bit of water has the highest sound? Try a favorite tune, and by changing the level of the water in each glass, you can change the tone it makes. Are you ready, maestro?

171. NUMBER CHARACTERS

 The plan: Make cartoonlike characters out of numbers that will fool nearly everyone!

What it takes:
- Plain white paper
- Pencil
- Eraser

A great way to start this activity is to write the numbers 1 through 10 on a piece of paper. Spread them out and write them big. You can always add them up and get an answer, but this number activity adds up to some very creative characters.

Turn the paper upside down and sideways. Hold it on an angle, and you can even try looking at the numbers with squinted eyes. Can you visualize the number 7 being the beak of a bird? Of course, you have to attach a bird to the beak, but you'll be able to do that and even more.

Now take a good look at the number 8. It could easily be the body of a person. Draw a head on the top; add arms, legs, and don't forget the shoes and other details. Turn the numbers any which way you'd like, and "calculate" which number you'll choose next. It will be fun to stump family members and friends when you show them your number characters and ask them to find the hidden number.

172. JACK'S BEANSTALK

 The plan: Make a towering beanstalk out of old newspapers that would make Jack proud!

What it takes:
- Old newspapers
- Scissors
- Transparent tape

Use a table or the floor, and open up one double-sided newspaper sheet. It will have a crease down the middle. Start at one side and *loosely* roll the newspaper to the center crease. Take a second open double-sided sheet of newspaper and lay it on the unrolled half of the first sheet so that it meets at the center crease of the first paper.

Now roll the rolled-up side over the new paper until you get to the crease of the second sheet. Stop right there, and place another double-sided sheet of newspaper over the last sheet. Roll up the same way: Roll the rolled-up side to the crease of the new sheet. Stop. Continue the same process over and over until you've rolled up at least ten sheets. Make sure you haven't rolled them too tight. Keep them loosely rolled. Next, tape the loose side of the last sheet to the roll so that you have formed a newspaper tube.

Use your scissors to cut five five-inch strips down from the top of one end of the newspaper tube. Stick your fingers down inside the top of the tube that you just cut, and carefully pull out the center part of the roll. Keep gently pulling and turning with your fingers at the same time, extending the length of the tube. Keep using this motion and pulling up until your newspaper tube has turned into a very tall beanstalk! Practice this paper trick, and get everything ready on a new beanstalk so you can astound your friends and family when you perform this trick before their very eyes!

173. TURKEY TALK

 The plan: Design and make a first-rate feathered gobbler out of a tracing of your hand!

What it takes:
- Piece of white paper
- Pencil
- Colored marking pens or crayons
- Glitter (optional)

Sit down at a table and place your hand on a piece of paper. Spread your four fingers apart, and move your thumb slightly away from the fingers. Take your pencil and trace around your fingers and thumb. This tracing will soon turn into a side view of a turkey! Can you see it now? You'll be able to turn those finger outlines into feathers as fast as you can say, "Gobble, gobble," and be sure you use your pencil to add more feathers between the "finger" feathers. Draw some feathers in front and some behind the "finger" feathers, and also sketch in a wing on the side. Round off the underside of the turkey, and add legs and feet.

Your thumb outline is going to be the turkey's head, and to make it look like a real gobbler, make the top of the head rounder, add a beak, an eye (only one since this is a side view), and of course, you wouldn't want to forget the floppy red fold that hangs down under the beak. This is called a wattle. Make your turkey look like the real thing by coloring it the best feather colors you can find!

174. A WHALE OF A TALE

 The plan: Make up the biggest, most outrageous whale of a tale you've ever heard!

What it takes:
- Lined paper
- Pencil

Think of the strangest, weirdest, most outrageous thing that could ever happen. Think *big*. Think about all the things in the universe that need to be explained, and then put your own "whale of a tale" thinking cap on and go to work. Write your own story. Remember, this is going to be a tall tale, which means you can exaggerate just as much as you'd like.

How would you like to *really* stretch the truth to explain what causes a volcano to erupt?

Why do frogs croak, or crickets chirp? Have you ever wondered why most ice-cream cones are cone-shaped? Why do you think cats like fish? Now's your chance to come up with an explanation for anything you'd like and to write a story about it. Take your pencil and write the title of your story across the top of the paper. Let your imagination go wild and those fingers fly! When you're finished, share it with your friends or family, and see if they don't think it's the craziest thing they've ever heard.

175. WINDSOCK

 The plan: Make a windsock to hang from a tree or a roof that will blow with the breeze!

What it takes:
- Scissors
- Empty round tube container like an oatmeal box
- White glue
- Colored construction paper
- Crepe paper or fabric
- Hole punch
- 4 12" pieces of string, and 1 18" piece

Use scissors to cut out the bottom of the container, and remove the lid. Next, you'll want to glue colored construction paper around the container so that it's completely covered. Using other colors of construction paper, cut out different shapes such as a sun, moon, and stars, flowers, ladybugs, jet planes, or anything you'd like, and glue them to the outside of the container. Make streamers out of crepe paper or even pieces of fabric, and glue them on the inside at one end of the container so they'll hang down.

Punch four holes in the opposite end of the container at the top. Be sure to space them evenly around the rim. Insert the pieces of string, one in each hole, and tie each one in a knot to attach it to the tube. Now take all four pieces of string and tie them together at the top where they meet. Tie another piece of string to the knot at the top, and this is what you'll use to hang your windsock on a tree branch or over a patio or deck.

176. LET YOUR FINGERS DO THE WALKIN'

 The plan: Your fingers become characters when you make one clever puppet out of gloves!

What it takes:
- Old light-colored glove
- Colored marking pens or tempera paint
- Scraps of yarn or embroidery thread
- White glue
- Paintbrush
- Scissors

Stick your hand in a glove and decide what fingers you want to use for your puppets. Maybe you'll want to use all four fingers and the thumb. If you decide on just one or two fingers you can glue the left-over fingers to the back of the glove so they won't show.

Use marking pens or paint on the fingers to make faces. You can glue on yarn or embroidery thread to make hair or mustaches, and don't forget the whiskers for your whiskered animals!

177. DESERT SANDS

The plan: Create a desert scene complete with cactus and look-alike sand!

What it takes:

- Brown paper grocery bag
- Scissors
- Pencil
- Colored marking pens or crayons
- White glue
- 2 bowls
- Water
- Paintbrush
- Cornmeal

Cut out a large section of the unseamed side of the grocery bag. Using a pencil on the unprinted side, draw a desert scene, complete with cactus and rocks, distant mountains, and maybe even a skull or two or an old prospector's shack. Use your marking pens or crayons to make your desert bloom with color. Think of the warm, sandy, desert colors of gold, orange, brown, yellow, and deep red. Maybe you'll even want to have a spectacular desert sunset.

When you've finished with coloring, squirt some glue into a bowl and add just enough water to make the glue a bit watery. Brush this glue and water mixture onto every area that you would like to see sand. Sprinkle cornmeal on top of the glue until the spots are covered. Wait about five minutes and then gently hold your picture over another bowl and let the excess cornmeal fall off into the bowl. Keep adding glue and more cornmeal until your picture looks just like a desert!

178. VISITORS WELCOME!

The plan: Write a travel guide to the place you know best . . . your own hometown!

What it takes:

- Piece of paper
- Pencil

What would people do if they came to your hometown or city for a three-day visit? What do you think would tempt anyone to visit and maybe even stay permanently? Here's what you do: Take a piece of paper and a pencil, and make headings across the top with titles such as PARKS, MUSEUMS, FAST-FOOD RESTAURANTS, ICE-CREAM STORES, LIBRARIES, and GOLF COURSES, to name just a few. Maybe your city has a BASEBALL STADIUM, or even a VIDEO ARCADE. What else does it have?

Write down the actual names of these hometown attractions underneath the headings, and it will be fun to see just what your city has to offer. At another time it might prove interesting to quiz family members and see just how well *they* know their hometown or city!

179. RUB-A-DUB DOILIES

 The plan: Turn those fancy and frilly paper doilies into an even fancier flower picture!

What it takes:
- Any size paper doilies
- Scissors
- 2 pieces of white paper
- Crayons

Those white and lacy paper doilies that you may have used in making Valentines in school are just what you need for this rubbing activity. Take your scissors and cut some sections out of a doily that look like a flower. There are sections that look like stars, and they will work nicely too. After you've cut out five flowerlike sections of different sizes, you're ready to become a paper doily florist.

Arrange the doily cutouts on a piece of paper so they resemble a bouquet of flowers or even a small garden. Next, place a piece of paper over the doilies. With the side of a colorful crayon, rub over one of the doilie flower sections.

Now pick another flower color and rub the crayon over one of the other doilie flowers. Keep doing this until you have a rubbing of all the doilie flowers. Remove the top paper and add stems and leaves with your crayons. Wow, what a garden!

180. CREATE-A-SPORT

The plan: Create a brand-new sport for the Summer or Winter Olympics!

What it takes:
- Lined paper
- Pencil

Everyone knows about the 100-meter race, high jumping, and pole vaulting. And when it comes to the Winter Games, the luge is always a favorite, along with speed skating and downhill skiing. Here's your chance to decide on a new, exciting event that athletes everywhere would love to compete in.

Think about ball games, or running races, or racket sports, or crazy jumping, sledding, swimming, rowing, running, throwing, leaping, and skating events that will excite the best sports kids in the world. Use a pencil to write the name of your event on a piece of paper, and then write a description of the sport along with the rules of the game. Who knows, maybe someday your idea may be an Olympic event!

181. FRAME YOUR FACE!

The plan: Make an animal cutout with *your* face in place of the animal's!

What it takes:
- About a 22"x 24" piece of white poster board
- Pencil
- Ruler
- Scissors
- Colored marking pens or crayons

In the center of the poster board use your pencil to draw an oval shape about six inches high and five inches wide. This space is where your face is going to fit, so you'll need to cut it out. Try placing your face behind the poster board in the opening to see if it frames your face. You may have to make a few more cuts to make the opening fit better.

Think of all the animals you can sketch in with your pencil, choose one, and then color the poster board around the hole with markers or crayons so that it looks like the head of the animal. A lion with a gold, orange, and brown mane might be a good wild animal to make, and a cat with whiskers, fluffy neck, and pink-lined ears would also look great. How in the world would you look as a grizzly bear, a panda, a gorilla, or a flop-eared rabbit? Remember, you're going to be the face of the animal! At a later time, you could even make several of these and then photograph your friends' faces in the animal frames for a fun, rainy day or birthday party activity.

182. SPOONER PUPPETS

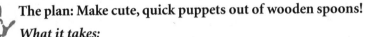 **The plan: Make cute, quick puppets out of wooden spoons!**
What it takes:
- Pencil
- Wooden spoons
- Permanent marking pens or tempera paint
- Paintbrushes
- White glue
- Odds and ends such as yarn, cotton, fabric, glitter, buttons, fake fur, raffia

Use your pencil to draw a face on the back side of a wooden spoon. Next, use marking pens to go over your lines, or paint over the pencil lines with a brush and tempera paint. You can put mustaches on your wooden puppets, and eyebrows and eyelashes. Of course, you'll want to make mouths, eyes, noses, and even ears. Glue on fake fur or yarn for hair. You may even want to "dress" your puppet by adding some fabric glued at the base of the bowl part of the spoon.

Don't just think you have to make people, because spoon puppets can be animals, too! Doll them all up with "extras" such as buttons for the eyes, cotton for an adorable lamb, or a headband of glitter for a rock star!

183. PRETZEL ORNAMENTS

 The plan: Turn ordinary pretzels into lacy tree ornaments!
What it takes:
- Aluminum foil the size of a piece of notebook paper
- Rounded type pretzels (not the sticks)
- White glue
- Ribbon or yarn

Place a sheet of foil on a table. Use several pretzels to make a design on the foil so that each pretzel touches another one. Where the pretzels touch, place a drop of glue to hold them together. You can make snowflake shapes, star shapes, circle shapes, and long shapes simply by hooking the pretzels together with glue. Let them dry overnight.

The next day, carefully pick your creations up off of the foil, and weave a ribbon in and out through the pretzel holes and tie it where the ribbon meets. You can place these directly on a tree by hanging them over the end of a branch, or you can tie on a separate piece of ribbon or yarn to make a loop hanger.

184. SOLO HANGMAN

 The plan: Play Hangman all by yourself!
What it takes:
- Paper or 3" x 5" index cards cut into 26 1" squares
- Scissors
- Pencil or pen
- 2 lunch sacks
- White paper

Write each of the twenty-six letters of the alphabet on twenty-six squares of paper. Separate the vowels from the rest of the letters. The vowels are *A, E, I, O, U,* and *Y.* Place them in a lunch sack by themselves. Put the rest of the letters of the alphabet in a separate lunch bag. Now you're ready to play Solo Hangman.

Draw the hangman's pole and noose on a piece of paper, then pick a letter from either bag. Since one letter won't spell anything, draw a "head" on the hangman's noose. The body will be a stick figure. Keep picking either from the vowel bag or the consonant bag until you can spell a word. When you pick one letter you can use it more than once in the word you're trying to spell. When you pick a letter that doesn't complete the word you're trying to make, you must add a body part under the noose.

As soon as you pick a letter that completes a word, you've won. See how fast you can spell a word without getting hanged!

185. SPIN A YARN

 The plan: Make a gorgeous yarn collage with yarn scraps and bits and pieces!

What it takes:
- White glue
- Colored construction paper or poster board
- Scissors
- Yarn scraps of many different colors

Take your glue container and carefully squeeze out some glue in any design of squigglies, squares, zigzags, or circles on a piece of poster board or construction paper. You can even make glue outlines of animals, people, and objects.

Cut yarn to fit the glue lines on the paper. Place the yarn over the glue line, and press down so that the yarn sticks to the glue lines. What kind of picture are you going to make? An abstract design? A landscape? You can even fill in the outlined areas with pieces of cut yarn. Glue the yarn inside the areas that you want to look solid.

186. PLEASE DON'T EAT THE PAINTING!

 The plan: Create the best-tasting picture you'll ever paint by using pudding!

What it takes:
- Large sheet of white paper, butcher paper, or tagboard
- Pudding cup that you buy at the store
- Spoon
- Washcloth

Be sure to wash your hands before you start one of the tastiest art projects ever. You can make an absolutely delicious painting by first placing your paper on a washable surface or table. Open up a cup of your favorite pudding and spoon it out onto the paper.

Now comes the fun! Use your hands and fingers to spread the pudding all over the paper, and then start drawing. You can squish and squeeze and even lick. Use a finger to draw, and guess what happens if you don't like what you've created? Right! Smooth the pudding over the paper, and start again!

You can let the painting dry if you'd like, or maybe you'll decide to eat the pudding right off the page!

187. TORN PAPER LANDSCAPE

 The plan: Create a spectacular paper landscape without using scissors!

What it takes:
- Assorted colors of construction paper
- 12"x 18" or any size light-blue construction paper
- White glue

No fair using scissors on this project, and you'll be surprised at what a beautiful landscape you can create by simply tearing the scenery! Start with the background first. Choose a piece of construction paper, and tear it into pieces that look like mountains or hills.

Glue them onto the light-blue paper. Place them about two inches down from the top of your paper. Next, tear some more mountains or hills in a different color. Glue them in front of the first mountains. Now tear some rolling hills to place in front of the two sets of mountains. Maybe these could be a shade of green.

If you'd like a lake in front of the mountains and hills, tear one that is long and narrow. How about some trees at the back of your lake? Tear tiny, thin tree trunks about the size of toothpicks, and tear tiny pieces of different shades of greens or even oranges and reds for a fall scene. Glue these onto your picture around the trees.

For the front of your landscape you could add a big tree or two with some large boulders. Tall grasses or bushes would also look terrific. When you're just about done, maybe two or three torn paper clouds above the top of your mountains will make your scene picture-perfect!

188. ANIMAL PARADE

 The plan: Use painted animal crackers to make a zany zoo or farm animal lineup!

What it takes:
- Animal crackers
- Colored poster board
- Tempera paint
- Paintbrushes
- Paper towel
- White glue
- Black fine-tip marking pen

Line up a whole menagerie of animal crackers on a piece of poster board. Get them in the order you'd like to see if they were parading right down the middle of your street. Now take one animal cracker at a time and paint it. Lay the painted animals out on a paper towel to dry. When they're dry, carefully glue them onto your paper in the order you decided on before. Use a black fine-tip marker to outline the other details of your picture. If you're worried about these critters being on the loose, you can always use a marking pen to draw them into a cage!

189. NOT ONLY FOR DRINKING

 The plan: Use a Styrofoam or paper cup to make a playful puppet!

What it takes:
- Any size Styrofoam or paper cups
- Pencil
- Colored marking pens
- Colored construction paper
- Buttons, movable eyes, fabric scraps
- White glue
- Popsicle sticks

Turn a cup upside down, and draw a face on one side of the cup with your pencil. Next, use your colored marking pens and trace over the pencil-drawn face. Colored construction paper, buttons, fabric scraps, and other odds and ends can be used to make hair, arms (glued on both sides of the cup), and features, or you can simply draw everything on with marking pens. Be colorful!

When your character has been cleverly created, all you need to do is glue a popsicle stick inside the front part of the cup. Leave enough of the popsicle stick showing below the edge of the cup, because this is where you're going to hold on to your puppet. Let everything dry before you have a dress rehearsal for the puppet show you can later present to your family or friends.

190. RAP IT UP!

 The plan: Be your own composer and make up a rap about anything you'd like!

What it takes:
- Lined paper
- Pencil

You've heard them. You know what they are. Now all you have to do is make one up on your own, and you can do that! Compose a rap! Do one about your favorite TV show, the family pet, your best friend, the cereal you eat for breakfast, or Aunt Judy's weird shoes! Be creative! Go wild!

> You can write a rap cause it's cool to do the beat
> Of the words that's in your head and the beat that's in your feet.
> You can snap your fingers as you try and rack your brain
> Or you can chug-a-chug chug like a choo-choo train.
> But you can write a rap since you now know how
> To put the words together; so smile and take a bow!

191. STICKER PICTURE

 The plan: Use colorful stickers and marking pens to create a marvelous sticker picture!

What it takes:
- Pencil
- Large piece of construction paper, butcher paper, or poster board in any size
- Stickers of people, animals, or cartoon characters
- Colored marking pens or crayons

Get out those old sheets of stickers and use them to make a colorful mural. Use your pencil to sketch in a scene on a piece of paper around the theme of your stickers. Sports, animals, cartoon characters, space travel, dinosaurs, cars, and food stickers are just a few of the sticker themes that you can use. Arrange the stickers on your paper, and then lick and stick or peel and stick them to your paper. Fill in the rest of your drawing with your marking pens or crayons to make a sticker picture!

192. MAGIC MESSAGE SPINNER

The plan: Make a spinner out of cardboard that sends a message every time it spins!

What it takes:

- Drinking glass or jar about 3" across
- Poster board or tagboard
- Colored marking pens or crayons
- Scissors
- Hole punch
- Ruler
- Pencil
- 2 rubber bands

Use a drinking glass or a jar, and place it on the poster board. Trace around it with your pencil, and then cut out the circle with your scissors. Punch two holes directly across from each other on the circle close to the edge. Think of a two-word message, like "Let's play." Use a marking pen to write one word on one side of the circle. Make the word big, fat, and bold.

Turn the circle over, and write the second word of your message so when you flip the circle over, the word will be *upside down* from the word on the other side. One part of the message will be on one side, and the other half of your message will be on the back of the circle.

Put the rubber band in one hole, and loop it through itself. Do the same with the other rubber band and the other hole. Pull tight on both rubber bands, and then by sticking your pointer fingers through the rubber bands, turn the spinner over and over to wind it up. When you let go, pull your hands apart a little and look at the spinner "spinning" to see your message. What are some other messages you could write? Happy Birthday? Good Luck?

193. PICK A NUMBER

The plan: Make a game that will sharpen your math skills as quickly as you can add 2 + 2!

What it takes:

- 3"x 5" index cards or plain paper
- Scissors
- Pencil or pen
- 2 boxes or baskets
- Paper

Cut the index cards in half or cut plain paper into four squares. Write numbers from 1 through 10 separately on the paper pieces. Do this three times so you'll have three sets of the numbers from 1 through 10. Each piece will have just one number. You'll have a total of thirty pieces of paper. Now place all these numbers in one of the boxes or baskets.

Write three plus signs (+), three minus signs (−), and three times signs (x) on different pieces of paper. You'll have a total of nine pieces of paper; now place these signs in the other box or basket.

To play the game, you select two numbers from the number box without looking, and one sign from the sign box. Do just what the sign says. If the sign is a minus sign (−), then you always subtract the smaller number from the larger number that you've picked from the number box. If it's a plus sign (+), just add the two numbers together. If the sign is a multiplication sign (x) simply multiply.

Don't forget to check your answers. The more you play the game, the better you'll get. You'll be surprised at how well you'll know your math facts!

194. ETCH-A-SKETCH IN FOIL

 The plan: An ordinary paper clip can etch a picture on foil treated with soap and paint!

What it takes:
- Piece of cardboard the size you want your picture
- Aluminum foil
- Transparent tape or masking tape
- Bowl
- Black tempera paint
- Liquid dishwashing soap
- Paintbrush
- Paper clip

Cover a piece of cardboard with aluminum foil. Wrap it around to the back on all four sides, and then tape it in place. Pour a little black or dark-colored tempera paint into a bowl, and add two or three drops of liquid dishwashing soap. Stir it with a paintbrush, and then brush the paint/soap mixture over the foil until it's covered.

When the paint is completely dry, open up a paper clip, and use one end of it to scratch or etch a picture or design in the paint. Be careful not to press down too hard or you'll tear the foil. Now that you know how to do this technique, try using different colors, and you can even try wrinkling up the foil before you tape it onto the cardboard for a very unusual effect.

195. STICK PUPPETS

 The plan: Attach a cardboard head to a stick and you've got a super stick puppet!

What it takes:
- Pencil
- Poster board or construction paper
- Scissors
- White glue
- Tongue depressors, popsicle sticks, craft sticks, tree twigs
- Old magazines or catalogs

Think of all the characters you can create when you make these quick and easy-to-make stick puppets.

Use a pencil to draw head shapes on the poster board or construction paper and cut them out. Keep them small, to fit on the sticks. Now attach them with glue about an inch down from the top of a stick. If you're using construction paper, cut two heads at the same time, and glue the stick between them. This will give the head more support.

You can cut faces of people or animals out of magazines and glue them to the poster board or construction paper, or you can design your own heads and color them in with marking pens or crayons before you glue them to the stick. Either way, these little stick puppets are so easy to make that you'll want to do all of the characters in your favorite story!

196. A TO Z

 The plan: Use the letters of the alphabet to create all kinds of silly characters!

What it takes:
- Piece of paper
- Pencil
- Colored marking pens or crayons

First, you'll need to decide just what it is you're going to draw. A person? An animal? A monster? An object? Next, you select any letter of the alphabet, and then write it on a piece of paper. Make the letter about two inches high. Turn the letter any which way you'd like, and then start adding the details.

Use your imagination, and draw a character that no one has ever drawn before. Think about all the crazy things you can add to your picture. Hats, jewelry, antennae, glasses, feathers, horns, or even a mask. Use your crayons or marking pens to finish your letter. Think polka dots, stripes, bright colors, or checks. Go wild!

197. THANKSGIVING CORNUCOPIA

 The plan: Make a "horn of plenty" that would make any Pilgrim's mouth water!

What it takes:
- Brown paper grocery bag
- Scissors
- Different colors of construction paper
- White glue
- Pencil
- Colored marking pens

Cornucopias or horns of plenty are a symbol of Thanksgiving. They're filled up with the fruits and vegetables of the harvest, and they look like a goat's horn. To make your cornucopia, cut a grocery bag into a horn-shaped cone. Make the mouth of the horn big because you're going to put lots of harvested paper "crops" in and around it. Make the other end pointy, like an ice-cream cone. Then gently bend the horn so it has a slight curve to it.

Place your cornucopia on a piece of light-colored construction paper and glue it on. Next, take your pencil and draw different kinds of fruits and vegetables on the construction paper and cut them out. Before you glue the fruits and vegetables into your cornucopia, arrange them and make changes until you have them looking just the way you want.

Some things you might want to include in your horn of plenty are small pumpkins, purple and green grapes (cut them out separately and arrange them in separate bunches), red and green apples, bright yellow bananas, nuts, squash, berries, cherries, and deep red cranberries. A few fall paper leaves sticking out here and there do lots to make it look like the Thanksgiving season.

198. LOONEY LIMERICKS

 The plan: Write your own funny little verses that have just five lines!

What it takes:
- Pencil
- Lined paper

Limericks are funny little poems that are probably named for a city in Ireland by the same name. Limericks have five lines. Lines one, two, and five rhyme, or end with the same sound and have about the same number of syllables or sounds. Lines three and four rhyme, or end with the same sound and have about the same number of syllables or sounds.

Here's one so you can get an idea how to do it:

There once was a house cat named Fred
Who learned how to stand on his head
He went on T.V.
And danced with a flea
And now poor Fred's scratching in bed!

A good way to begin a limerick is to start out with, "There once was . . ."

Try this outline and see if you can make up a limerick. If you can do this one, then you're definitely ready to try one on your own!

There once was _____

Who _____

She _____

With _____

And _____

199. REFLECTION PERFECTION

 The plan: Make a watery reflection of a scene that will look like the real thing!

What it takes:

- Drawing paper
- Old newspapers
- Scissors
- Pencil
- Watercolor marking pens
- Paintbrush
- Water
- White glue
- Transparent tape

Fold a piece of drawing paper in half the long way. Now cut the drawing paper in half. Place both halves on the newspapers. On one of the halves, use a pencil to sketch a scene that you might see at the edge of a body of water. It could be a landscape of a lake, or a town on the banks of a river. Color in the scene with watercolor marking pens. Now take your paintbrush and cover the other cut half of the drawing paper with water. Place the scene you've drawn at the top of the paper covered with water so that the cut edges match up. The colored picture will be directly above the half that you've just covered with water.

Now draw a reflection of your scene on the wet piece of paper below, using the watercolor markers. Make sure that you use the same colors for the objects in the reflection that you used in your picture. The lines will run and look watery just like a reflection looks on water. When the reflection is dry, you can glue or tape the two pieces together to make a complete picture.

200. APPLE PEOPLE

 The plan: Carve peeled apples to make faces, and then turn them into charming old people!

What it takes:
- 1 or more peeled apples
- Teaspoon
- Salt
- Fresh or bottled lemon juice
- Bowl
- Paper towel
- Pencil
- 1 or more long-necked bottles
- **Optional:** • Beads • Fabric scraps • Cloves • Old makeup • Fake hair • Old glasses • Tempera paint

Hold the peeled apple in one hand and, with the tip of the teaspoon, carve out the features of a face. Carve spots on the apple for two eyes, a nose, and a mouth. Shake a little salt into a bowl with the juice of one lemon, or two tablespoons of bottled lemon juice. Place the apple head in the bowl, and add enough water so that it is covered with the liquid. When the apple is soaked with the lemon-salt water, remove it from the bowl, and dry it off carefully with a paper towel.

Take the pencil and push it into the bottom part of the apple like a popsicle. Place the pencil with the apple on it into a long-necked bottle, and let the apple dry out in a warm place for three weeks. Keep checking on your apple face, because it's going to wrinkle and shrivel up to look like a very old person. You could do three apple faces at one sitting, and then choose the one you like best after they've shriveled and shrunk, or use them all.

After the three weeks you can have a whole new activity when you fill in some of the indentations. You could use beads or cloves for the eyes. You may want to paint the mouth with some red tempera paint and add clothes that you make out of fabric scraps to make your apple person a real sight to behold!

201. CLEAR AS A PICTURE

 The plan: Spiff up your favorite book with a bookmark that you've created and covered!

What it takes:

- Colored construction paper or poster board
- Ruler
- Pencil
- Scissors
- Yarn
- Colored marking pens or crayons
- Stickers (optional)
- Clear contact paper
- Hole punch

Nothing looks better in your favorite book than your own personal handmade bookmark. Use your ruler and pencil to measure and mark a piece of construction paper or poster board about 6" x 2", or you can make your bookmark any size or shape you'd like. Cut it out.

Using your crayons or markers, you can decorate it any way you'd like, and adding stickers would really make your bookmark fancy. Measure off a piece of contact paper that is more than twice as large as your bookmark. Place the bookmark facedown on one half of the sticky side of the contact paper and press down. Now fold the unstuck part of the paper over the side of the bookmark facing you. Press down so that the contact paper is stuck to the bookmark. Use your scissors to trim around the edges, leaving about a one-fourth-inch margin all the way around.

If you really want to make your bookmark look like the ones in the stores, punch a hole near the top end with the hole punch. Next, you can thread a piece of yarn through the hole and tie it. Can you think of a favorite book for your new bookmark?

202. SPARKLE AND GLITTER

 The plan: Make a sparkling design with water, glue, and lots of glitter!

What it takes:
- Old newspapers
- Bowls enough for each color of paint
- Piece of cardboard or poster board
- White glue
- Tempera paint
- Pencil
- Paintbrush
- Spoons
- Glitter

Spread old newspapers on a table, and place the cardboard or poster board on the newspaper. Use a pencil to lightly sketch a design or a picture on the cardboard. Mix a few squirts of white glue and the same amount of paint in a bowl and stir. Use a different bowl for each of the colors and glue you want to use. Paint your picture with a brush, using the glue and paint mixtures. Now all you have to do is sprinkle glitter over the wet glue mixture, and when it dries gently tap the paper to shake off the extra glitter. You'll have a sparkling picture!

203. BUTTERFLY BEAUTY

 The plan: Design a beautiful butterfly whose wings are tissue-paper thin!

What it takes:
- 2 pieces of 12" x 18" black construction paper
- Ruler
- Pencil
- Scissors
- Tissue paper of different colors
- White glue

This butterfly with the delicate tissue-paper-thin wings will look like it can take flight when you finish making it. First, fold one piece of black construction paper in half the long way. Lay your ruler on the fold. Draw a line along the fold and down the outside edge of your ruler. This will be the center of your butterfly. Draw the wings of your butterfly by starting about two inches down from the top of your ruler line. Make curving pencil lines that start at the ruler line, go toward the edge of the paper, then down, ending two inches up from the bottom of the ruler line.

Cut out around the curving lines. Round off the top and bottom of your fold line. Open the paper and see what improvements you can make so the wings look more like real butterfly wings. Fold the paper over again, and draw oval or round areas on the wings. Cut out the inside of each oval shape, keeping the paper still folded. Now open up the butterfly and place it on top of the second sheet of black paper. Trace around the edges and in the holes of the cutout butterfly, and cut the second butterfly out. Place different colors of tissue paper over the holes you've cut on one of the butterflies, and glue them on. This will be the wrong side of your butterfly. When all of the holes are covered with tissue paper, lay the identical butterfly over the one with the tissue paper. Glue this in place, and now you've got a beautiful butterfly!

204. SIX SIDES

 The plan: It will be snowing indoors when you learn to make these six-sided snowflakes!

What it takes:
- Pencil
- 4 different-size plates or saucers
- White 8½" x 11" copy-machine paper
- Scissors

Did you know that all snowflakes have six sides and that no two of these beautiful crystals of ice are ever alike? To make a paper snowflake, trace around a plate or saucer on a piece of white paper to make a circle. The next step is to cut out the circle, and fold it in half. Hold the folded paper so the folded side is on the bottom, and fold it in thirds so that the left side overlaps the right. You end up with a folded circle that now looks like the shape of a slice of pizza. If you unfold it now you will see that it is in six sections.

Fold it back up again and make little cuts with your scissors on both sides of the "slice." When you unfold it you will see that you've just created a six-sided snowflake! Make several of these using different-size plates for the circle pattern.

The more little cuts you make, the lacier your snowflake will be. Go ahead and experiment. Maybe you'd like to tape your flakes to a window or have an adult help you pin them carefully on a curtain. However you display your snowflakes, you can be sure that these crystal-looking creations won't melt!

205. OVER AND UNDER

 The plan: Make an obstacle course right inside your house for those rainy indoor days!

What it takes:
• Large ball of string or yarn

Take your shoes off. Now hold the ball of string or yarn in your hand and start in any room of your house. Begin the obstacle course by tying the end of the string to the leg of a piece of furniture.

Carry the ball of string from one room to the next, and go under tables, over and around sofas (be careful not to walk on furniture), behind the TV, under the bed, around the lamp, in and out of the chair legs, and on and on and on.

Be clever, and go in and out, around and about, and into places that even the dog wouldn't want to go! When you get to the end of your rope (string or yarn), simply stop and tie the string to another chair leg somewhere in your house..

Finally, go back to the beginning where you tied the string to the leg of a chair, and now you can rewind the string and retrace your steps until you come to the end, or you can go from the end to the beginning. You could even set up the course for someone else to do! Make sure everyone in your house knows what you're doing—you don't want anyone tripping over your obstacle course!

206. DO NOT DISTURB!

The plan: Design a doorknob sign that sends a message to all who want to enter!

What it takes:
- Poster board or construction paper
- Colored marking pens or crayons
- Drinking glass or jar
- Ruler
- Pencil
- Scissors

Can you think of different messages to write on a doorknob hanger? DO NOT DISTURB is one message that everyone knows. GENIUS AT WORK, COME IN, OUT FOR LUNCH, QUIET, COMPUTER WHIZ, and BEWARE OF MONSTERS are a few more suggestions, but you can probably think of something even better. Give it a try. When you've got one in mind, it's time to make your doorknob hanger.

With your ruler or without, draw a rectangle about four by eight inches or larger on a piece of poster board or construction paper with a pencil. Cut it out. Place a drinking glass or jar on the rectangle, and trace around the bottom for the hole where the doorknob will fit. Make the hole near the top of your rectangle. Cut out the paper inside of the hole. Try your doorknob hanger on a doorknob to see if it will fit. You may need to cut the hole a little larger. Use your marking pens or crayons to decorate your hanger and write the message. How about BATMAN IS IN?

207. COMMERCIAL BREAK

The plan: Make up and write your *own* TV commercial!

What it takes:
- Lined paper
- Pencil

What's your favorite commercial? What does it say? Why do you like it? When you answer these questions you're well on your way to becoming your own advertising agency and writing your own commercials!

Pick a product. Any product will do. How about Honda, Cheerios, Big Macs, Snickers, Power Rangers, or M&M's? Think about what makes some advertisements stand out in your mind. When you're in the advertising mood, pick up your pencil and paper, and start jotting down ideas for a dynamic commercial.

Hints: Say something to get people's attention. Ask a question or make a statement about the product. Describe the product. Tell why your product is *the* best. You could even say why it's better than the competition. End with a bang such as a clever jingle, slogan, or saying, like "Got Milk?" "Just Do It," or "Betcha Can't Eat Just One!" Now it's your turn!

208. COTTON SWAB COLLAGE

 The plan: Use the tips of cotton swabs to make a three-dimensional picture!

What it takes:
- Pencil
- Colored poster board the size you want your picture
- Scissors
- Cotton swabs
- White glue
- Black fine-tip marking pen

Draw a picture with your pencil on a piece of poster board of something that is usually mostly white, or black and white, or dark and light. How about some sheep, a penguin, a zebra, a kitten, a rabbit, a snowman, a daisy, or a white rose? You could even draw a tree or two topped with snow on the branches.

Use scissors to cut the tips off of cotton swabs. Glue the cotton swab tips touching each other on the parts of your picture that are white. If you're drawing more than one of the same subject such as a few sheep, select just one of the sheep to be three-dimensional. Add the finishing touches and details with a black fine-tip marking pen, and you'll have yourself a unique three-dimensional picture.

209. PEEK-A-BOO

The plan: Create a scene in a shoe box that has a hole in one end, and take a peek!

What it takes:

- Shoe box
- Scissors
- Ruler
- Colored construction paper
- White drawing paper
- Colored marking pens or crayons
- White glue
- Small objects you want to use for the scene

Take the top off the shoe box. Cut a hole that's about one and a half inches across in the center of one end of the box. Now build a scene inside the box facing the hole. You can make scenery out of construction paper that you cut into shapes such as trees and mountains, or you can draw scenery on white drawing paper and use marking pens or crayons to add color. Attach scenery pieces to the sides or back of the box by gluing a small piece of sponge to the back of the object. Then glue it to a spot on the inside of the box.

Glue some small objects in the box. Use scissors to cut a hole about two inches by two inches in the center of the lid of the box. This will let the light in so you can see the scene better. Place the lid on the box, and tape it into place. Now, take a peek!

210. SPONGE PRINTS

The plan: Use sponges cut up into different shapes to make the most creative prints ever!

What it takes:

- Sponges of any shape, size, or texture
- Scissors
- Tempera paints in different colors
- Dishes for the paint
- Drawing paper or butcher paper
- Warm water and soap

Use your scissors to cut up the sponges into any shape you'd like. Hearts and flowers, half moons and stars, baseballs and bats, apples and leaves, or even the letter initials of your name will make excellent sponge printers. Pour a small amount of different colored paint into separate dishes. Dip one side of the sponge into the paint, and then press the paint side onto your paper. Lift up the sponge quickly so it doesn't run.

Butcher paper printed with your sponges makes excellent wrapping paper, especially when you repeat the print over and over. You can even change colors on the sponge you're using, but wash out the sponge with warm water and soap before you place it into a different color. Be sure to keep the colors all separate. Think of all the things you can sponge paint!

211. LOTS OF DOTS

 The plan: Make up your own connect-the-dot pictures for others to enjoy!

What it takes:
• Plain white paper   • Pencil

With your pencil make a simple line drawing on a piece of plain paper. Think about the connect-the-dot pictures that you've done in the past, and you'll remember that they were usually simple line drawings. Some good ideas for a picture might be a rabbit, a bird in a tree, a boat in the ocean, a vase of flowers, a person on a surfboard, a football going over the goalpost, a butterfly sitting on a leaf or . . . ? You decide!

Now that you have your drawing, start by placing the number 1 somewhere on the picture. Next write a number 2, 3, 4, and so on until you have outlined the drawing with numbers. Remember that the lines will all be connected between the numbers, so you must write the numbers in order.

When you have all of the numbers on your drawing, it's time to place the numbers on a blank piece of paper. Place a blank piece of paper over the drawing with the numbers and write the numbers only on the top sheet. If you can't see through the paper, place both pieces on a window in the daytime and the light shining though will help you see the picture and the numbers.

The finished product is a sheet of paper with numbers on it! Do you already know who you're going to give this to?

212. PINECONE FLOWERS

The plan: Make wood flowers with pinecone petals and twigs!

What it takes:

- 3 or more pinecones
- Old newspaper
- White glue
- Small twigs
- Pods, nutshells, or seeds

Break the petals off of a pinecone and place them together in a circular pattern so that they overlap and touch each other on a piece of newspaper. Glue the petals together, and let them dry. Glue a small but sturdy twig on the back of the flower for the stem. Next, find a pod or half of a nutshell, and glue it in the center for the finishing touch. You could also use a little bunch of seeds or kernels for the center of your flower. Can you make a whole bouquet?

213. PICNIC PUPPETS

The plan: Those picnic paper plates and bowls make great puppets!

What it takes:

- 2 white paper plates or 2 paper bowls
- Stapler
- Ruler
- White glue
- Pencil
- Colored construction paper
- Marking pens
- Odds and ends such as yarn, buttons, sequins, beads, and ribbon

Staple two paper plates with the fronts facing each other together at the edges. Leave a space wide enough for a ruler to be inserted at the bottom, *or* glue the edges together, still leaving the ruler space. Sketch the features of your character's face on one plate with a pencil. Then use cutouts of colored construction paper, or use your marking pens to finish the face of your puppet character.

Old buttons can make a great nose or eyes, and you can even glue yarn on the back plate and some on the face plate for hair. If your paper plate puppet is a girl, she'd probably like a ribbon in her hair. Make a bow, and glue it on. Now all you need to do is insert the ruler in the space you left open, and you've got a puppet ready for the next performance. It's showtime!

214. TRAVELING ARTIST

 The plan: Roam the outdoors with cardboard and glue, and create a picture as you go!

What it takes:
- Sneakers
- Heavy piece of cardboard
- White glue

Put on your sneakers and go for a nature walk around your yard or neighborhood with a piece of cardboard and a bottle of glue. Pick up interesting natural objects as you walk, and glue them onto the cardboard. It will be fun to show people what the traveling artist created when your picture is dry and ready to be displayed. Ideas: Leaves, pods, grasses, flower petals, weeds, seeds, twigs, stems, bark, and small rocks.

215. LICK AND STICK!

 The plan: Design your own colorful, eye-catching postage stamps!

What it takes:
- White drawing paper
- Pencil
- Colored marking pens
- Black fine-tip marker
- Scissors

What would you like to see on a postage stamp? Rain forests and birds, deserts and insects, or even space shuttles and jets are all possible designs for a brand-new postage stamp. Who knows, maybe someday one of your creations may actually be a winning design.

Doodle a few ideas with a pencil on a piece of paper first, and then decide on the one you're going to turn into a stunning stamp. You can look at a real stamp to see how they are supposed to look. When artists design stamps their pictures are very large, but they are then reduced to the size of a postage stamp.

You can use any size white drawing paper for your stamp design. Some stamps are perfectly square, and others are rectangles turned longways or rectangles that go up and down. Make your design crisp and colorful with not too many fine details.

If you're making a U.S.A. stamp be sure that the letters U.S.A. are on it. Stamps are many different prices, so make yours like the real ones of thirty-two cents or more. Of course, you can't mail letters with your make-believe stamps, but they look terrific on envelopes holding letters or notes you're going to hand-deliver to someone!

216. FAT YARN ORNAMENTS

 The plan: Use glue and water to make shapes that will turn into stiffs overnight!

What it takes:

- Waxed paper
- Pencil
- White glue
- Bowl
- Water
- Paintbrush
- Fat yarn such as rug yarn
- Scissors

Spread a piece of waxed paper on a table, and use a pencil to draw an object on the waxed paper. The drawing will be light. All lines in your design must touch or your ornament will fall apart after it's dry. All lines have to be somehow connected. Next, squeeze white glue into a bowl, and add enough water so you'll have two parts glue to one part water. Stir with a paintbrush.

Try to measure the amount of yarn you'll need by placing it all around the outside edge of your design. Now soak the yarn in the glue and water mixture. When you pull it out, use your thumb and pointer finger to squeeze some of the glue mixture out and back into the bowl. Lay the glued yarn over the outline of your design on the waxed paper. Keep repeating this process with all the other lines, making sure that each piece of yarn overlaps another piece so they will stick together.

If you use double or triple outlines of yarn, the design will be even stronger. Let the designs dry overnight. Remove them from the waxed paper the next day, and they'll all be stiff as a board and ready to hang!

217. COVER UP

 The plan: Make your own CD or cassette cover to replace the old one!

What it takes:
- Plastic CD or cassette holder
- Pencil
- White drawing paper
- Colored marking pens or crayons
- Black fine-tip marking pen
- Scissors

CD and cassette paper covers are easy to remove from their plastic cases. The first step is to take the paper cover out of a CD or cassette case, and trace around it on a piece of white drawing paper with a pencil. Lightly trace the lines where the cover folds. Now's your chance to come up with an even better design than the original. Use a pencil to lightly sketch in some graphics and any words.

You may want to change the name of the CD or cassette completely, and since you're in charge, you can do that! The next step is to color everything in with your marking pens or crayons. It might be a good idea to do any lettering with your black fine-tip marking pen.

The last step is to cut out your cover, fold it, and insert it in the plastic CD or cassette holder for a whole new look.

218. LOTS OF DOUGH

 The plan: Make your own play dough that you can turn into great sculptures!

What it takes:
- Old newspapers
- Large mixing bowl
- 1 cup flour
- ½ cup water
- Spoon
- Tempera paint

Place all of *What it takes* on newspapers, and then mix up a batch of this baker's dough. In a large mixing bowl place one cup of flour and add one-half cup of water. Stir to mix well. To color the dough, add a few drops of tempera paint until you get the color you want. Use your hands to mix everything up, and if the dough is sticking to your hands, all you have to do is add a little more flour. You can pound it, push it, pull it, hit it, beat it, squish it, and then shape it into a wonderful work of dough art! Let your sculptures dry overnight to harden.

219. SPIN IT!

 The plan: Make a pinwheel that will turn into a real spinner in the wind!

What it takes:
- Colored construction paper or lightweight poster board
- Ruler
- Pencil
- Scissors
- White glue
- Straight pin
- Another pencil with an eraser

Cut a square out of the construction paper or poster board that is six inches on all sides. Use a ruler to measure. Fold one corner to the opposite corner and unfold. Now fold the remaining corner to the other opposite corner and then unfold. You now have four creases that meet in the middle of your square. Put a dot in the center.

Use your scissors to cut on the four crease lines up to about one inch from the center point. Don't cut all the way through to the center.

Now take every other corner and bring it to the center point. Don't fold it down tight or crease it. It should overlap a little in the center. Hold the corners and push a straight pin through the middle, connecting the four layers.

Roll up a little piece of leftover paper into a tiny ball about the size of a kernel of corn, and glue it so that it will keep its shape. When the glue is dry, push the pin with the pinwheel on it through the ball, too. To make a stick to hold your pinwheel, take your pencil with the eraser, and push the pin with your pinwheel and the little ball on it into the side of the eraser, but not all the way through. Be careful not to stick yourself. Now all you need is a little breeze, and you'll have yourself a spinning pinwheel.

220. ROCK CRITTERS

 The plan: Create rock critters that may (or may not) look like the real animal!

What it takes:
- A variety of different-size smooth rocks
- Pencil
- Black fine-tip marking pen
- Paintbrush
- Tempera paint
- White glue
- Yarn, fake fur, movable eyes, sequins, beads, buttons

Even if you have a *real* pet, you may still be interested in another pet that doesn't have to be walked, fed, or put out at night!

Select a rock whose shape could resemble an animal. Use your pencil or black a fine-tip marking pen to draw on features such as the mouth, nose, eyes, and ears. Now draw on the body. The next step is to paint over and around your pencil lines with a brush using tempera paint.

Dress up that critter by gluing on yarn hair, fake fur, movable eyes, or anything else that makes this animal one you'll want to keep indoors. And just what are you going to name this new pet?

221. LET IT SNOW!

The plan: Use cotton and white paint to make this snowy wonderland of a picture!

What it takes:
- Dark-blue construction paper
- Pencil
- White tempera paint
- Paintbrushes
- White glue
- Cotton balls

Sketch a simple winter scene with your pencil on the dark-blue paper. Decide where you want to place the snow. Think about having snow on mountaintops, rooftops, and treetops. Maybe you'll have snow around a lake or pond, or even on a fencepost. Use white tempera to paint your picture. In about five minutes when the paint is dry, squeeze some glue onto the areas of snow that you want to stand out, and then place the cotton over the glue. You may have to stretch the cotton to fit some of the spaces.

If you'd like to make your picture look like it's *really* snowing, use the tip of the glue container to make tiny dots of glue in the sky. Don't forget that snow falls on trees and over houses and ponds. Is it going to be snowing in your picture?

222. LIFELINES

The plan: Use a line to make a word and picture story of your life!

What it takes:
- White drawing paper
- Pencil
- Black fine-tip marking pen
- Marking pens or crayons

Place the tip of your pencil on the upper-left-hand corner of your paper. Now draw a curving, lazy-looking line that covers the whole page but does not cross over itself. End up in the bottom-right-hand corner of the paper. At the starting point write your birth date. At the ending point write today's date.

Use your pencil or fine-tip marking pen to write words and draw pictures on or next to the line that tells about *you* from the time you were born until right now. You may want to use words like *baby*, *stroller*, *Ma-ma*, *crawling*, and *walking*, in between pictures of things that show what you did.

You could even draw a picture of a baby bottle, a crib, or your very favorite blanket. The last words and pictures should be about you today. When you finish, you can add some color to the pictures on your Lifeline!

223. KING ARTHUR'S CASTLE

 The plan: Paint six milk carton castles and use them as bowling pins.

What it takes:
- Old newspapers
- 6 1-quart milk cartons
- Tempera paint
- Liquid detergent
- Small bowl
- Paintbrush
- Small rubber ball

Spread old newspapers over your work area. Paint the six milk cartons to look like thin castles. If you want your castles to be gray, mix white paint with a tiny amount of black paint in a bowl. A few drops of liquid detergent will make the paint stick to the milk cartons. Paint some black windows and a door on each castle. Then let them dry.

While the paint is drying, clean up your mess and find a spot large enough for a "short bowling alley," maybe outdoors on the cement. At one end of your "short bowling alley" set up the six castles: three on the back row, two on the middle row, and one in front.

Walk to the opposite end of your "short bowling alley" and roll the rubber ball toward King Arthur's castle. The challenge is to knock all the castles over with one roll. Good luck! If it is too easy, roll the ball from farther away.

224. MARCHING BAND

 The plan: Make a marching band from empty toilet paper rolls!

What it takes:
- Empty toilet paper roll for each band member
- Tempera paints
- Nail
- Pipe cleaners
- Paper clips, paper circles, piece of clay, toothpicks

Marching band members all look alike and have uniforms, so paint tall hats, faces, shirts, belts, and pants that look alike on each empty toilet paper roll. Be sure to paint all the way around each roll. Let the paint dry.

Using a nail, carefully poke a hole on each side where the arms attach. Push a pipe cleaner through the two holes for arms.

Make band instruments for the pipe cleaner arms to hold. Bend paper clips to form a trombone or a trumpet. Small paper circles look great for cymbals. A round piece of clay could be a drum. A toothpick makes a baton. Attach the instruments on the pipe cleaner arms and bend the pipe cleaners so it looks like the instruments are being played by your marching band!

225. CODE CRACKERS

 The plan: Create your own secret code for writing secret messages!

What it takes:
- Pencil
- Lined paper

Spies use private, coded messages to pass along their secrets. You can make up your own secret code, just like a spy. First, write the alphabet (A, B, C, D, etc.) across the top of your paper. Give each letter a number, and write it underneath the letter. It's best not to make "A" the number 1 or your code will be too easy to solve. Maybe you could begin with "D" as number 1, "E" will be number 2, "F" is 3 and so on. Finally the letter "A" will have the number 24, "B" is 25, and "C" is 26. Got it?

Now think of a special message you would like to send. How about inviting a friend to your house for a special "code" making party. You could write:

26-12-10-2 17-12 10-22 5-12-18-16-2 24-11-1 10-24-8-2
16-2-26-15-2-17 26-12-1-2-16. 6-17 20-6-9-9 25-2 3-18-11.

You are a smart Code Cracker if you read it right. When you send a code message to your friend you might hint that "D" is number 1 (or whatever letter you decide is number one) so the code is not too hard to crack.

226. FOREVER GREEN

 The plan: Create a modern art Christmas tree design!
What it takes:

- Two contrasting colors of construction paper
- Pencil
- Scissors
- White glue

Fold one piece of construction paper in half, the long way. On the folded half draw half of a Christmas tree. Then inside the first drawing, draw four or five other trees following the outline of the first tree.

Cut out each tree, starting with the largest tree. Do not cut the fold. When finished you should have four or five tree-shaped rings. Open them up. Carefully take out every other ring and set them aside.

Arrange the trees you have left, one inside the other, on the piece of contrasting color construction paper. When it looks just right, paste the trees down. Now you have an unusual yet striking Christmas tree design.

227. GREAT GIFT TAGS

 The plan: Make gift tags for all gift-giving occasions!

What it takes:

- Several 3" x 5" index cards or pieces of white construction paper
- Used greeting cards from birthdays and holidays
- Used wrapping paper from all occasions
- Scissors
- Glue stick or white glue
- Small box
- Black marking pen

You can be ready with a special gift tag for the presents you wrap and give to friends. Fold each of your three-by-five cards or three-by-five construction papers in half so they look like little books, and set them aside. These folded cards will become the gift tags. Now look through the used greeting cards and wrapping paper for figures or shapes to decorate the tags. You could cut out balloons and birthday cakes, Valentine hearts, Christmas trees and bells, Easter baskets and bunnies or flowers, and any other shapes. When you think you have enough decorations, carefully cut them out, and glue them onto the first page of the folded tags. The inside of the gift tag is for writing a message and signing your name when you are ready to give a gift.

Write "Gift Tags" on the small box with a black marking pen. Store your decorated gift tags in this little box, and when you want to send a special gift to someone your gift tag will already be made.

228. NUTTY-BUG

 The plan: Create a ladybug from half of a walnut shell!
What it takes:
- 1 half walnut shell
- Small piece of brown paper bag
- Pencil
- Scissors
- White glue
- Orange and black tempera paint
- Paintbrush
- Moveable plastic eyes

Place a half walnut shell open side down on a small piece of brown paper bag. Trace around the shell edge with a pencil. Cut out the tracing. This piece will cover the open side of the walnut shell. Run a line of white glue along the open edge of the shell. Glue the tracing onto the shell. Let it dry for a few minutes.

Turn the half walnut shell over. Paint the shell orange. When it is dry paint a thin black line lengthwise down the middle of the shell. Now the shell looks like it has two wings. Paint a few black dots on both wings. At one end of the shell paint a small black head. When the paint is dry, glue on two plastic eyes.

Your **Nutty-bug** is ready to place on a windowsill or in the dirt at the base of a houseplant as soon as the glue and paint dry.

229. CHRISTMAS SHOPPING WISHES

 The plan: Search through old catalogs for family Christmas gifts!
What it takes:
- Piece of paper
- Pencil
- Old catalogs (Penneys, Sears, Best, or others)
- Scissors
- Glue stick

Here's the greatest way to do some make-believe Christmas shopping. Fold pieces of plain paper in half. Write the name of each person on your shopping list at the top of each half: Mom, Dad, Grandma, Grandpa, Sister, Brother, Friends, and even your pet. Write only one name on each half piece of paper.

Get out an old store catalog that shows pictures of everything. Now let your fingers do the shopping for each person on your list. When you find something that's just right, cut it out and glue it under the person's name. Great shopping! Isn't it fun to pretend?

230. PINPOINT PICTURE

 The plan: Pin-prick a picture, hold it over a lighted lamp, and see the picture light up!

What it takes:
• Old magazines
• Scissors
• 9" x 12" poster board
• Glue
Old newspapers
Straight pin

Cut out a picture you like from an old magazine. Glue it to the poster board. Place the poster board on a thick stack of newspapers to protect your furniture. Prick holes with a pin around all the details of your picture. Space the pin holes evenly.

Place your pinpoint picture over a lighted lamp shade and see it light up!

231. SOUPER DOOPER

 The plan: Create an ABC picture using alphabet pasta!
What it takes:
- Pencil
- Colored marking pens or crayons
- 1 bag of alphabet pasta
- Small piece of waxed paper
- Plain white paper
- White glue
- Pie tin or paper plate
- Tweezers

Draw a simple picture with your pencil on the plain white paper. You can draw a tree, snowman, flowers, a rocket sailing to the moon over your house, or wherever your imagination takes you. Color the picture with colored marking pens or crayons.

Now pour a handful of the alphabet pasta onto a pie tin or paper plate. Search through the pasta bits until you find the letters that spell the picture you have made. If you drew a rocket ship, find the pasta letters that spell ROCKET SHIP. Squeeze a glob of glue onto the waxed paper. Use the tweezers to dip one letter at a time into the glue, and glue the pasta letters onto the picture. Now find pasta letters for all the other things in your picture and glue them in place, or draw another picture and start all over again. Are you a good speller? This will give you lots of extra practice. Be sure you've spelled the words right before you glue!

232. SILLY SCENE

 The plan: Use old odds and ends to make a silly picture!
What it takes:
- Old wrapping paper, used greeting cards, wallpaper, old magazines
- Scissors
- Piece of white paper
- Glue stick or white glue
- Black marking pen

Look at old wrapping paper, used greeting cards, old wallpaper scraps, or old magazines for people, animals, objects, and weird shapes that could be used to make a very silly picture. Cut out these items, and glue them on the white paper, mixing up all of the items to make a Silly Scene. When you have completed your scene, let it dry, and then finish it by outlining some of the shapes with a black marking pen.

233. ANCHORS AWAY

The plan: Be an "anchor" person by recording the news on a tape recorder!

What it takes:
- Pencil
- Lined paper
- Newspaper
- Cassette recorder
- Cassette tape

Has anything exciting happened in your neighborhood today? News anchors gather news from many sources, and you are about to become a news anchorperson. Maybe the neighbor's cat chased your parakeet. Maybe an old tree blew down in a storm. That's news! Use a pencil to write it on your lined paper so you won't forget.

Take a look at the newspaper. What does the headline (the biggest black print on the front page) tell you? Is it the kind of news story you want to report? Look at the other stories in the newspaper. Jot down some news items you would like to report. Look at the sports and weather pages. Who's playing in the Super Bowl? Will it rain or snow? Write it on your paper.

Now decide which of your news items should be reported first. Look at your list. Give each a number according to its importance. The most important item should be reported first.

Now get out the tape recorder. Check your cassette tape to be sure it is working. Start by announcing the date and then identify yourself as the "anchorperson." "Good evening. It's January first, and this is Gayle Goodheart with the news." Then start talking! Use your news item list to keep the broadcast running smoothly. This will be great to share with family and friends!

234. DESIGNER PAPER DOLLS

 The plan: Draw a paper doll and create your own designer clothes for the doll!

What it takes:

- White construction paper
- Colored marking pens or crayons
- Wallpaper scraps
- Ruler
- Pencil
- Scissors

Take your pencil, measure six inches, and draw a six-inch doll in a swimsuit on white construction paper. Color the doll and swimsuit with colored marking pens or crayons, then cut the doll out.

Now you can create top fashion clothes for this doll. First place the doll on top of a piece of construction paper or wallpaper. With the pencil trace lightly around the doll's shape where clothing would fit. Trace around areas for pants, a shirt, a dress, or whatever article of clothing you want to design. When you remove the doll from the paper you will have an outline to fit the doll. Fill in all the designer details and then color your designs.

Draw tabs on the shoulders and sides of the paper clothing that when folded over will fasten the clothes to your doll. Cut the clothes out with the tabs, and you are ready to dress your doll in your designer creations.

235. STUFFED SNOWMAN

 The plan: Create a spunky snowman by stuffing a plain old white sock!

What it takes:

- Cotton batting or cotton balls
- Scrap of material for a scarf
- 2 small colored buttons
- Scraps of black and other colors of felt
- Old white sock
- Rubber band
- White glue
- Bits of yarn

Stuff a white sock with cotton batting or cotton balls, but leave two inches unfilled at the opening. Wrap a rubber band around the spot at the opening where the stuffing ends. Fold over the top two inches like a cuff to make a hat. The heel of the sock will be the snowman's face and the foot will be the body. Take a scrap of material and tie it like a scarf below the heel to separate the head from the body.

Glue two small buttons on the face as eyes. Cut out the rest of the snowman's features from pieces of black felt. You can glue a felt belt, hat, vest, or any other piece of clothing onto your snowman. Stand your creation on a windowsill looking out, of course!

236. ALL IN THE FAMILY

The plan: Design a family flag!

What it takes:
- White drawing paper
- Pencil
- Colored marking pens or crayons
- Scissors
- Extra-large piece of paper
- White glue

Nations have flags. Countries have flags. Cities have flags. Even the Red Cross has its own special flag. Important groups have flags to let you know they exist. Your family should have a flag, too. Get out a paper and pencil and start thinking. What does your family do? Where do your parents work? Think of something important about your family and draw it with a pencil on the drawing paper. If your dad builds houses, you could draw a hammer and nails. Maybe your mom works at home or in an office. Draw something she uses in her work every day. If your family likes to go camping you could draw a tent and a tree. Draw something you and your brothers or sisters like to do. Make sure each thing you draw is quite simple. Look at the things you have drawn. Color everything in bright, bold colors, and carefully cut out each item.

Get out the extra large piece of paper. It will be your "flag." Decide how the cutout items can be arranged to form a good-looking flag. Glue everything down when it is just right. Fly your family flag proudly!

237. SUPER STAR

 The plan: Make a Christmas star ornament using toothpicks and construction paper.

What it takes:
- Yellow construction paper
- Pencil
- Scissors
- Hole punch
- Colored round toothpicks
- White glue
- String

Here is a very easy-to-make Christmas decoration. First, draw a star shape with a pencil on yellow construction paper and then cut it out. Punch a hole one-half inch from one star point (this is where the string will go). Take your colored toothpicks and glue one to each side of the star's points. Let the pointed ends of the toothpicks extend beyond the edges of the star. You can break the toothpicks before gluing if you want to have shorter points. Be sure to glue toothpicks around all of the star points. Tie the string through the hole when all the glued toothpicks are dry, and hang your star on a Christmas tree, a cabinet pull, or a doorknob. You could even make several and hang them outside on the branches of a bush.

238. SNAP, CRACKLE, AND POP

 The plan: Invent a new cereal name and design a box to go with it!

What it takes:
- White drawing paper
- Pencil
- Colored marking pens or crayons
- White glue
- Empty old cereal box

Get out your paper, pencil, and "thinking cap." What would you put on a new cereal box? A bright bowl full of cherry red alligators and hippos? Lightening bolts? Muscle men? Draw your new designs on a piece of paper with a pencil and color them with marking pens or crayons.

What will you name the new cereal? Write the new name in big, bold, colorful letters. When you are finished writing and coloring, glue your artwork onto an old cereal box. Trim the edges. How about it? Is your new box a winner?

239. MILKY WAY MAGIC

 The plan: Create a stand-out space picture of brilliant colors with a black background!

What it takes:
- Old newspaper
- White construction paper
- Crayons
- Black tempera paint
- Plastic bowl
- Water
- Paintbrush

Cover your work area with newspaper. On the white construction paper draw a space picture with crayons. Make a sun, Earth, stars, rocket ship, comet, maybe even people standing on the moon! Color everything several times over so the colors are bright and thick.

Pour some black tempera paint into a plastic bowl, and add a little water until the mixture is quite thin so that it will cover the paper but not the drawing. Using the paintbrush, paint the entire picture with the thin black paint. The background is black and the bright colors really stand out! It looks like real outer space!

240. FIND YOUR WAY HOME

 The plan: Make a personal map showing how to get to your home.

What it takes:
- Map of your city or community
- Pencil
- Piece of paper
- Ruler

Have you ever been far away from home and felt lost? Here's an easy way to find your way home. First, think of a place that is quite far away from your home like the mall, fairgrounds, or downtown. Look on the map and find the location of that far-away place and make a light pencil dot on it. Now look for where you live on the map and make a light pencil dot on the spot.

Now get out your paper. Beginning at the faraway place, use your finger to trace the way to your home. Write the street names and which turn (right or left) should be taken to get to your home. On another piece of paper draw a street map to show how to get from the far-away place to your house. The ruler will help you make the streets straight. Label the far-away place on your map, as well as each street, and of course, your house. It's a great feeling when you can find your way home!

241. ART HEARTS

 The plan: Create beautiful pictures with all shapes, sizes, and textures of hearts!

What it takes:
- Paper scraps of tissue paper, newspaper, wallpaper, butcher paper, contact paper, wrapping paper
- Scissors
- Construction paper
- White glue
- Colored marking pens or crayons

Cut out many different sizes of hearts on all different kinds of paper. Fringe the edges of some hearts. Make wavy edges on other hearts, or cut designs on them. Now arrange the hearts on a piece of construction paper. You can make all kinds of patterns and pictures with the hearts, such as flowers, animals, people, or even spaceships. Glue them down when you are happy with your picture. You can use colored marking pens or crayons to outline and draw more hearts. How interesting that the word "art" is part of the word "heart!" It doesn't have to be Valentine's Day to give someone this special creation!

242. PENCILS' DELIGHT

 The plan: Make a pencil holder from an orange juice can!

What it takes:
- Orange juice can
- Leftover wallpaper piece (at least 9" high and 12" wide)
- Pencil
- Ruler
- Scissors
- White glue
- Small bowl
- Water
- Paintbrush

Cover the orange juice can with the piece of wallpaper. Use your pencil, ruler, and scissors to trim the wallpaper so that it's just the right size. Glue the wallpaper to the orange juice can.

Now pour about one inch of white glue into a bowl. Thin it with one teaspoon of water, and stir well with a paintbrush. To make your covered can look smooth and shiny, paint it with the thinned glue mixture. When it is dry the glue coating will protect the wallpaper covering and give it a real professional look. Your beautiful pencil holder will be a great gift for Mom or Dad, or you may like it so much you'll want to keep it on a shelf or desk in your own room.

243. RIGHT ON TARGET

 The plan: Make a felt target, put Velcro strips on Ping-Pong balls, and try to hit the target!

What it takes:
- 12" x 12" piece of heavy felt
- 3 different sizes of round bowls
- Black permanent marking pen
- 3 Ping-Pong balls
- 3 rough adhesive Velcro strips, ½" wide

On the 12" x 12" piece of felt, make a target by tracing around the three different-sized bowls with a black marking pen. First, place the largest bowl on the felt, then trace around it. Next, take the smallest bowl, and place it evenly inside the large circle. Then trace around this bowl. Now take the medium bowl, place it between the two circles and trace again.

Place a strip of rough, adhesive-backed Velcro around each Ping-Pong ball.

Place the felt target on the floor, stand back several steps, and throw the Ping-Pong balls at the target. When you get to be a good shot, step back a little farther and test your skill again!

244. CUPS AND MARBLES

 The plan: Play baseball by shooting marbles toward blocks surrounded by paper cups!

What it takes:
- 4 small pieces of paper
- 4 toy blocks or pieces of wood
- Pencil
- Transparent tape
- 10 small paper cups
- 3 marbles

A very small baseball game can be played right on your floor all by yourself. Start by preparing the baseball diamond. On the small papers write first, second, third, and HR (for home run). Tape one paper to the top of each block. Set the blocks in a half circle about one foot apart with first on the right and HR on the left; second and third go in between.

Between each block place a paper cup on its side with the open end facing you. Put a paper cup (on its side) in *front* of each block. Place the last three paper cups in the spaces *behind* the blocks.

Put a piece of tape on the floor about two feet in front of the cups and blocks. This piece of tape is the "batter's box." The baseball diamond looks more like a fan than a diamond! Now you're ready to play ball!

The object of this game is to pitch (roll) the marbles from the "batter's box" and hit one of the blocks. If you miss and the marble goes into a cup, you're out. If you miss and the marble does not go into a cup, it's a strike. Three strikes and you're out. You can make up your own rules or use baseball rules. Pretend you're in the World Series! Batter up!

245. SHOE-BOX TRAIN

The plan: Make a train from shoe boxes.

What it takes:

- Shoe boxes (as many as you want)
- Nail
- String
- Tempera paint
- 1" paintbrush
- Paper clips

Collect some old shoe boxes. These will be the cars for your train. Carefully punch two small holes with a nail on the short ends of each box near the bottom. The two holes should be about the length of a paper clip apart in the center of the end sections. Cut off two pieces of string for each box about the length of four paper clips. Thread a piece of string through each set of holes and tie the ends together to make a small loop.

Paint your boxes to look like the cars of a train. Make an engine by painting a box black. When it's dry, paint an engineer's window on both sides and big silver or gray wheels. Box cars have big sliding doors on both sides and can be painted any bright color you wish. The caboose is painted red, of course. Paint the lids of the boxes to match the cars, but don't glue them down. When you want to put cargo in your train, just lift the lid!

Pull paper clips apart so they look like an "**S**" shape. These are the train's "couplers." Hook the paper clip ends into the string loops tied near the bottom of each box. Cut off a long piece of string and tie it to the front of the engine so your shoe-box train can be pulled.

246. HOW MANY CAN THERE BE?

 The plan: Fill jars with beans, cotton balls, and macaroni for a family guessing game!

What it takes:
- 3 small jars the same size with lids
- Bag of dried beans
- Bag of cotton balls
- 3 pieces of wrapped candy
- Pencil
- Piece of paper
- 3 pieces of lined paper
- Bag of macaroni

Prepare a guessing game for your family and friends that will be ready whenever they want to play. First, remove the lids from your three jars, and set your pencil and paper by the first jar. Now open the bag of dried beans and begin counting as you drop beans into the first jar. It will be easier if you count one handful of beans at a time, and then write that number on your paper. When the jar is just about full, add up the total number of beans you have put in the jar. Circle this number on your paper and write "beans" above the circle. Replace the lid.

Now repeat the same thing with the cotton balls and the macaroni, putting them in separate jars. Remember to count carefully, and record the number for each jar. Hide this paper so no one but you will know the right numbers.

Now that your jars are all full, get out the lined piece of paper. Write "beans," "cotton balls" and "macaroni" at the top of the paper. In the margin leave room for names of people who play your guessing game. When you are ready to play, show the players the three jars, and let them guess how many items are in each jar. Have them write their guesses on the lined paper. The person who guesses closest to the right number wins the grand prize of a piece of candy!

247. PAPER STRIP PUZZLES

 The plan: Cut out eight strips of poster board and use all eight strips to make puzzle shapes!

What it takes:

Ruler, pencil, scissors

- 8" x 2" strip of poster board
- 7" x 2" strip of poster board
- 6" x 2" strip of poster board
- 5" x 2" strip of poster board
- 4" x 2" strip of poster board
- 3" x 2" strip of poster board
- 2" x 2" strip of poster board
- 1" x 2" strip of poster board

Use a pencil and a ruler to measure and mark the eight strips of poster board. Cut them out and try to make the following shapes from the eight strips of poster board. *All eight strips must be used in making each shape,* one at a time.

#1 Make two rows exactly the same length

#2 Make three rows exactly the same length

#3 Make four rows exactly the same length

#4 Make a staircase with eight steps.

#5 Make a staircase with four steps.

#6 Make a staircase with three steps.

#7 Make a pyramid.

#8 Make a bridge—several types of bridges can be made. How many can you make?

#9 Make a rectangle.

Can you make any other shapes using all eight strips?

248. ROOM ABC'S

 The plan: Make a personal ABC book from items found in the house!

What it takes:
- 26 pieces of plain white paper
- Crayons or colored marking pens
- Pencil

On the first piece of paper take a pencil and write a big letter *A*. Turn that page over and write a big *B* on the next piece of paper. Continue writing one letter of the alphabet on each piece of paper until you've gone from *A* to *Z*.

Here comes the fun! Look around the room and find something that begins with *A*. Maybe an apple, an afghan, or an alligator (dead, of course). Draw a picture of the *A* word on the *A* paper. Go on to the *B*, *C*, and *D* pages. Find something *in the room* beginning with that letter and draw it. When you get to the hard letters like *Q*, *X*, and *Z*, you might have to look in the kitchen or even the attic. Color in your pictures. Good hunting and drawing. When you finish you will have a very personal ABC book.

249. PEEL-A-WAY FROZEN FRUIT CUPS

 The plan: Mix up a delicious frozen fruit treat in paper cups!
What it takes:
- 1 banana
- Mixing bowl
- 2 cups plain yogurt
- Small paper cups
- 3 tablespoons frozen orange juice concentrate
- Table knife
- 1 tablespoon brown sugar
- Mixing spoon

Good cooks always assemble everything needed for a recipe, so wash your hands thoroughly with soap and water, and get out *What it takes*.

Peel the banana and cut it into small chunks with the table

knife. Put the chunks into a mixing bowl. Add the yogurt, orange juice concentrate, and brown sugar. Stir until all the ingredients are well mixed.

Fill small paper cups, not quite to the top, with the mixture. Place the cups in the freezer. It takes about eight hours for Peel-A-Ways to freeze, but they are worth the wait! Never use a spoon to eat Peel-A-Ways. Instead, tear the paper cup away as you bite off mouthfuls. It's lots more fun then eating it with a spoon!

250. GIVE A CLUE

 The plan: Create a guessing game by writing clues to find hidden objects!

What it takes:
- 11 pieces of lined paper
- Pencil
- Envelope

Prepare this game for your family. When they get ready for some fun your Give a Clue game will be all ready to pull out and use!

Write the numbers 1 to 10 down the side of a piece of lined paper. This will be the "key paper." Now select ten objects in your home: photograph album, washing machine, perfume, and so on. List the ten objects on the "key paper." For example, #1 photograph album, #2 washing machine, #3 perfume. Continue this for all ten items you selected.

Now number each of the ten remaining pieces of lined paper, pages 1 through 10. On page number 1 write a clue about #1 from the "key paper." The clue might say, "People stare back at you from this object. It is kind of heavy. We like to look at its pages." Of course, these are clues for the photograph album. Now write clues for each of the ten objects on separate pieces of paper. Remember, don't write the name of the item on the clue page. Fold all eleven sheets of paper and put them in an envelope marked Give a Clue. At a later time, get out the envelope and stump your family!

251. ANCESTOR TREE

 The plan: Draw a tree showing who your family ancestors are!
What it takes:
- White construction paper
- Pencil
- Black fine-tip marking pen
- Old photograph album
- Colored marking pens or crayons
- Scissors
- White glue

When you draw this Ancestor Tree it will remind you of your wonderful family background. Using a pencil, lightly draw a tree trunk on the white construction paper. Lightly write your name on the trunk. Draw two branches coming off the trunk. Write your mother's name on the left branch and your father's name on the right branch.

Draw two branches coming off your mother's branch and write her parents' names on each of these. Draw two branches coming off your father's branch and write his parents' names on these. These people are your grandparents. Do you know the names of your great-grandparents? If you do, make branches for them coming off of the grandparents' branches on both sides. Now go over the tree lines and names with a black fine-tip marking pen.

Look through old photograph albums for pictures of these people. Draw and color a little picture of each person. Do your best to make your pictures look like the photographs. *Do not use real photos.* Cut your drawings out and glue them on the proper branch. What a family! What a tree!

252. PAINTING BY HAND

 The plan: Create a work of art by using your hand as the paintbrush!

What it takes:

- Big old shirt to cover your clothes
- Saucers (one for each color)
- Pieces of white drawing paper
- Black fine-tip marking pen
- Old newspapers
- Tempera paints
- Large bowl of water
- Old rag

Cover your clothes with a big old shirt, and cover the work area with old newspapers. Pour a small amount of tempera into each saucer. Set a piece of white drawing paper on your newspapered work area and start painting. Your hand is now a paintbrush! First, dip just a finger or two in the paint and see how it looks on the white paper. If you want to test different prints of your hand on the old newspapers, it's all right! Use fingers, sides of your hands, thumbs, fists, knuckles, and pinkies. The bowl of water and old rag can be used when you change colors. Tree trunks and branches are easy to make with the side of your hand, and leaves are about the size of your pinky.

When your painting is completed and dry you might want to add some details with a black marking pen. Your signature on the painting will look good, too! Are you ready to try another one?

253. PICTURE THIS

 The plan: Use pictures in place of words to liven up any short, short story!

What it takes:

- Lined paper
- Pencil with an eraser
- Old magazines
- Scissors
- White glue
- Stickers

People have done REBUS writing for years. It sounds complicated, but it's really just a combination of symbols and pictures and letters and numbers and drawings of things in place of words. Make up a very short, one paragraph story in your mind. Now take your pencil in hand and write the story on the lined paper.

You can cut pictures and letters out of magazines and glue them on, use stickers, or draw symbols yourself. Begin erasing words that can be replaced in your story. For example, if you wrote, "I ate . . . ," you could draw a picture of an *eye* followed by the number *8*. The word "before" could be replaced with the letter *B* and the number *4*. How could you do, "The sun was behind a cloud?" Simple! Draw a picture of a sun or cut and paste one on the paper, and for "behind" you could do a letter *B*+hind. Draw a cloud, and you've got a REBUS sentence. You may want to make a final copy, leaving more space for your symbols. R U red+E 2 go?

254. SNOWMAN MOBILE

 The plan: Build a snowman mobile that will brighten any cold winter day!

What it takes:
- White construction paper
- Circle forms (3 different sizes) for tracing
- Pencil
- Scissors
- Ruler
- String
- White glue
- Cotton balls
- Construction paper scraps

This snowman mobile is great to watch twist and twirl in your room during the winter months.

Use a pencil to trace around three round bowls of different sizes on white construction paper. Cut the circles out and arrange them like a snowman leaving one inch of space between each circle. The small circle goes on top, then the middle size circle, and the biggest circle is on the bottom.

Use a ruler to measure a piece of string about six inches longer than the snowman. Squeeze a line of glue down the center of each circle. Lay the string along the line of glue. Leave about six inches of string at the top for hanging your snowman mobile. From paper scraps cut out eyes, nose, mouth, buttons, and a top hat. Glue the pieces on the snowman. Glue the hat to the string a half inch away from the snowman's head. When the string is dry, glue cotton balls all over each circle on both sides.

When all the glue is dry, hang your snowman mobile where it will catch a little breeze or air from a heat vent.

255. SECRET LETTER

The plan: Write a message by adding a secret letter to the end of each word!

What it takes:
- Pencil
- Lined paper

There are lots of ways to write secret messages. This code is quite simple if you know the *secret letter,* and you can choose any letter you want. For right now the secret letter will be *H,* and here's how the code is done.

Write a message and add H to the end of each word: COMEH TOH MYH HOUSEH ONH MONDAYH. (Of course, it says, "Come to my house on Monday.")

Write all the words of the message, plus the secret letter, as one long word: COMEHTOHMYHHOUSEHONHMONDAYH.

Now, divide the message into three letter words: COM EHT OHM YHH OUS EHO NHM OND AYH.

Practice writing lots of messages. When you get ready to send a secret message, you will have to whisper the secret letter to your friend.

256. ON A CLEAR DAY

 **The plan: Create mirror and window pictures with
window cleaner!**

What it takes:
- Spray bottle of window cleaner
- Old newspapers

Spray art is "in" all over town, and it can be "in" in your own home, too, when it's put to good use. Everyone will be happy if you practice this art form often. Grab a bottle of window cleaner and find a mirror or window. One that needs a good cleaning is best. Decide what kind of picture (or message) you want. Now just begin to spray. It's kind of like drawing with a paintbrush.

When the picture is finished, wad up a sheet of newspaper and thoroughly rub away your artwork. Rub in the corners, too. If it "shines like glass" you've done a great job. Choose another mirror or window to practice your spray-paint technique again. Practice makes perfect. Wow! If you practice drawing on every window and mirror in the house you'll be the best-loved artist in town. Your mom will thank you most if all the used newspapers are thrown in the recycling bin when you're done.

257. SOAPSUDS PAINT

 **The plan: Mix up detergent and liquid starch to create
bubbly paints for pictures.**

What it takes:
- Old newspapers
- Mixing bowl
- 1 capful of liquid detergent
- 2 tablespoons of liquid starch
- Hand-operated eggbeater
- Brown wrapping paper or bag
- Plastic containers
- Tempera paints
- Water
- Spoon
- Scissors

Cover your work area with old newspapers. In a mixing bowl add one capful liquid detergent and two tablespoons liquid starch. Beat the mixture with an eggbeater until the mixture is about as thick as cake frosting. You are now ready to color the soapsuds paint, so decide what colors you want. Spoon the suds into a separate plastic container for each color. Next, add a few drops of paint to each container and stir with a spoon. Clean the spoon with water between colors. There should be enough suds for three pictures.

Cut open a brown bag or spread out the brown wrapping paper. Your fingers are the paintbrush, so dip into one color and begin. If you want a darker color, add a little more paint. If the soapsuds paint gets too thick, add a little more starch and stir it in with a spoon. You'll "feel" terrific when you do this painting!

258. COLOR SEARCH

 The plan: List everything in your house that is a certain color to discover a color winner!

What it takes:
- Lined paper
- Pencil
- Ruler

Are you a good color detective? Here's a way to find out. First, select eight of the most used colors in your house. Then choose four colors and write them across the top of a piece of lined paper with a pencil. Using the ruler, make four columns, one for each color listed. Use a second piece of paper for the other four colors, and make columns.

Now, start the color search. Quickly begin looking for something in your house that is one of the chosen colors. Write the things you find in the column under that color. If one of the colors chosen was black, you might write "toaster handles" under the black column. Go, go, go! How many items did you list in each color column?

259. HALLOWEEN SPRING THING

The plan: Make a Halloween mobile from construction paper!

What it takes:

- 6" x 6" piece of orange construction paper
- 6" round bowl
- Black construction paper
- Transparent tape
- Pencil
- Scissors
- Hole punch
- Black thread

Place a round bowl on the orange construction paper. Use a pencil to draw a line around the bowl. Cut the circle out. Make the circle into a spring by drawing a continuous circular line starting at the edge of the cut-out circle and making smaller and smaller circles until you reach the middle. Your circle lines should be about one-half inch wide.

On the black construction paper draw and cut out little Halloween figures about two inches tall, such as cats, jack-o'-lanterns, spooks, witches, and bats. Near the top of each figure, punch a hole with the hole punch.

Pull open your circle spring. On each spring layer punch a hole with the hole punch. Tie a piece of string onto each hole. Tie the other string ends onto the black Halloween figures. Attach your Halloween spring thing over a doorway with transparent tape or outside on a tree.

260. STAND-UP CHRISTMAS TREE

The plan: Decorate a cutout Christmas tree that stands on a paper cylinder!

What it takes:

- Piece of paper
- Green poster board
- Pencil
- Scissors
- Fabric scraps, buttons, sequins, rickrack, foil
- White glue
- Empty toilet paper cylinder

You can make a beautiful stand-up Christmas tree that is just the right size for your room. Fold a piece of paper in half. Draw half of a Christmas tree with a pencil from the fold line and cut it out. Use this as a pattern to trace around on the green poster board. Cut out the tree and decorate it with the scraps you have collected. Cut the toilet paper cylinder in half and make a one-inch slit on both sides of one end. Slide the Christmas tree into the slit and the Christmas tree will stand.

261. FOR YOUR EYES ONLY

 The plan: Write invisible messages on wet paper. Read the messages by wetting it again.

What it takes:
- Dry towel
- Mirror or window
- Water in a large mixing bowl
- 2 pieces plain white paper
- Ballpoint pen

Place a dry towel under the mirror or window you are using. Decide what message you want to write. You could even draw a picture.

Fill a mixing bowl halfway with water. Quickly dip one piece of paper into the water. Carefully smooth it onto a mirror or window. Place the dry piece of paper over the wet one and write your short message on the dry paper with a ballpoint pen. If your message is long, the ballpoint pen may stop giving out ink, but don't worry, the message will still come through on the wet page. Take the dry paper off and throw it away so no one will know what it says. You will be able to see the message clearly on the wet paper, but as it dries, the message will completely vanish.

With the towel wipe up all the watery drips you've made. When the wet paper is dry it will fall off of the mirror or window. When you want to read the invisible message, dip the paper in water again!

262. CRAZY CREATION

 The plan: Name the crazy creation *before* **you glue scraps of paper onto a paper plate!**

What it takes:
- Paper plate
- Black marking pen
- Scraps of colored construction paper
- Scraps of fabric
- Scissors
- White glue

Along the bottom of the paper plate write, "This is a _____" with a black marking pen. Fill in the blank with a crazy name for the crazy creation you are going to create. Some wacky names like Ziggy-bop, Goochnik, Twirpey, or Klukpup would be really weird.

After you've given the plate a name, start cutting and gluing scraps of construction paper and scraps of fabric onto the plate until you have a really crazy creation. Don't glue anything over the crazy name. Hang it on the wall and you'll laugh every time you look at it.

263. DRESS UP A FRIEND

 The plan: Make paper dolls out of magazine pictures!

What it takes:
- Old magazines and catalogs that advertise clothes
- Scissors
- Poster board
- White glue
- Old photograph of a friend

Dressing like the "rich and famous" is a dream come true in this activity. Look through old magazines and catalogs until you find a beautiful "whole body" picture of a man, woman, or child (all three if you want). Carefully cut your picture or pictures out. Glue the figures onto a piece of poster board. Cut the figures out of the poster board.

Your paper doll can really be your friend if you cut out the face of one of your friends from a photograph. Paste your friend's face over the face of the paper doll. You might even paste on a photo of your own face.

Every paper doll needs a wardrobe of clothes. Search through the magazines again to find new outfits for your doll to wear, like swimsuits, pajamas, raincoats, tuxedos, and evening dresses. Cut these clothes out. Cut little tabs on both shoulders of the clothes you cut out. These tabs can be folded over your paper doll's shoulders to hold the piece of clothing in place.

When you've cut out a whole wardrobe of clothes, it's time to dress up a friend. Take your "friend" on a holiday to the beach, a night on the town, or business at the office. Go to places you've only dreamed of. Play make-believe with a "friend" paper doll even if the friend is *you*!

264. NO PEEKING

 The plan: Find and list twenty-five items for your family to identify blindfolded!

What it takes:
- Lined paper
- Pencil
- 25 small household items (paper clip, stuffed toy, pencil, etc.)
- Large paper bag
- Handkerchief, scarf, or necktie to use as a blindfold

Write the numbers 1 to 25 along the margin of the lined paper with a pencil. Find twenty-five small items around the house nobody uses, things that might be hard to identify if you were blindfolded. Next to the #1 on the lined sheet of paper, write the first item and drop it into the large paper bag. Now choose another item for #2, #3, and so on until you have written all twenty-five different items and dropped them into the paper bag.

When all the objects are in the bag, tie a blindfold over your eyes, and reach your hands into the bag. Feel one at a time. Can you identify them? Some are kind of hard to guess, right? When you have identified all the objects put them back into the paper bag along with the list you made and the blindfold.

Next time you and your friends get together or your family is looking for something to do, just pull out your "No Peeking" bag. See if they are good at identifying the objects. Everything you need for the game will be in the bag. As a blindfolded player pulls an object out of the bag, check the items off when they are identified correctly.

265. FAMILY ALBUM

 The plan: Draw family members and place them in a special folder!

What it takes:
- White construction paper; a piece for each family member
- Pencil
- Colored marking pens or crayons
- Folder

Use your pencil to draw and then color a big picture of one member of your family on white construction paper. Draw that person doing something he or she really likes to do. Write that person's name at the bottom of the drawing. Remember the kind of clothing he or she wears. Repeat this for each member of your family.

Place all the pictures in a folder and write "Family Album" on the outside. When you show it to your family you might cover the names and have them guess who it is. Don't forget to draw yourself!

266. FELT FUN

The plan: Create a bookmark made of felt!

What it takes:
- Ruler
- Pencil
- 3" x 8" piece of felt
- Scissors
- Felt scraps in assorted colors
- White glue

Use a ruler to measure and a pencil to mark a 3" x 8" piece of felt. On one end cut a curve, or a point, or one inch of fringe. This fancy edging is the bottom of your bookmark.

Cut out designs from the scraps of felt such as a giraffe, an apple tree, a bunch of bright flowers, or any object that will fit on the bookmark. Glue the felt designs to the bookmark. You can use this beautiful bookmark for yourself or give it to a friend!

267. HOPSCOTCH SNAIL

The plan: Draw a snail-shape hopscotch and play the game!

What it takes:
- Large smooth cement area
- Sidewalk chalk

On a large, smooth cement area, draw twenty squares that are larger than a big shoe that circle inward to form a snail shape. Number each square, starting with #1.

To play the hopscotch snail game hop on your right foot (without stepping on any lines or falling down) from square #1 to square #20. Change to your left foot and hop back to square #1. If you step on a line or fall down, you must start again.

With some practice you could be the best hopscotch snail hopper in your family!

268. ART BOX

 The plan: Cover a box and fill it with all kinds of art supplies!

What it takes:

- Box and lid (big enough to store your art supplies)
- Wrapping paper or large grocery bag
- Scissors
- Transparent tape
- Black marking pen
- Art supplies like colored marking pens and crayons, pencils, erasers, glue, popsicle sticks, paper, tempera paint, scissors, and other items

Set your box on a smooth area and wrap it with either wrapping paper or a large grocery bag. Use the scissors to get the paper the right size. Wrap the lid separately. Tape down all the loose edges, and then with your black marking pen write "Art Supplies" in big letters on the side of the box.

Now all you do is gather your art supplies and put them in the box. It will really be great to have all of these items in one place when you're ready for them. All you have to do now is find a good storage place for the box!

269. FINE TO FEEL

 The plan: Create a picture with fabrics of different textures!

What it takes:

- Small pieces of fabric that feel smooth, rough, bumpy, silky, stiff, limp, furry
- Bits of yarn, string, ribbon
- Scissors
- Colored construction paper
- White glue

Search around your house for old pieces of fabric (cloth) with different textures. Texture means the way things feel: smooth, silky, rough, and so on. Also look for pieces of ribbon, yarn, and string.

They have texture, too. When you have found many textures of cloth and ribbon, use the scissors to cut the pieces of cloth into different shapes. Animal or automobile shapes would be fun, or you could cut squares, circles, diamonds, and triangles. All of these textures will be fine to feel when your picture is completed.

When all the shapes are cut, arrange them artistically on a piece of construction paper. The shapes can overlap each other or they can stand alone. Use the bits of yarn, string, or ribbon to give variety and additional texture to your work of art.

Once you decide where the pieces go, glue them to the construction paper. While your masterpiece is drying, clean up all the leftover bits and pieces.

270. BUG IN A NUTSHELL

The plan: Create a funny bug using half a walnut shell!
What it takes:
- Old newspapers
- Half of a walnut shell
- Tempera paints
- Paintbrush
- Scissors
- Decorating scraps of fabric, ribbon, beads, sequins, beans, pasta, foil, and other bits
- White glue

Cover your work area with old newspaper. Paint the half walnut shell any color you like, and let it dry. Cut out eyes, nose, mouth, feelers, feet, arms, or whatever things your bug might need from the decorating scraps. Glue your decorations to the painted shell and make it as cute as a "bug in a rug"!

271. COTTON BALL SNOWMAN

 The plan: Build a snowman with rolled-up newspaper and cotton balls!

What it takes:
- 7 whole pages of old newspaper
- 5 rubber bands
- White glue
- Small plastic bowl
- Paintbrush
- A very large bag of cotton balls
- Pencil
- Colored construction paper
- Scissors

Stack the seven pages of newspaper one on top of the other and fold along the center fold mark. Roll the papers from bottom to top to form a cylinder. Secure the cylinder with five rubber bands.

Pour white glue into a small plastic bowl. Hold the cylinder upright, and with the paintbrush, coat one section with the glue. Quickly press cotton balls onto the section until it is completely covered. Repeat this procedure with other sections until the cylinder is completely covered with cotton balls. Leave the bottom of the cylinder open.

This snowman should have a round head at the top of the cylinder, so dip cotton balls into the glue and add them to the top of the cylinder until a round head forms. Add more cotton balls to the bottom section until there is a fat, round body. It will take lots of cotton balls.

Draw eyes, nose, mouth, buttons, scarf, and hat with a pencil on the construction paper. Glue these to your cotton ball snowman. When he dries he will make a good winter decoration for your home.

272. VALENTINE STREAMERS

The plan: Create heart streamer decorations to hang over a doorway or window!

What it takes:
- Pink and red construction paper
- Yarn (red, pink, white, or black)
- Transparent tape
- Pencil
- Scissors
- Ruler

Draw with a pencil and then cut out dozens of pink and red hearts from pink and red construction paper. Make them all different sizes, but not too big. Then cut ten pieces of yarn, all different lengths, but none longer than eighteen inches. Tape the hearts one at a time to the yarn you have cut. Each piece of yarn should hold many pink and red hearts.

Tape the ten Valentine streamers over a doorway or in front of a window. They will look great for the whole month of February.

273. PRESS ON!

The plan: Transform a brown paper bag into a fall tapestry by doing a leaf rubbing!

What it takes:
- Leaves, twigs, grass, petals
- Old newspaper
- Brown paper grocery bag
- Scissors

Gather a leaf collection in your yard, and while you're at it, pick up any twigs, grass, and flower petals that look interesting. Spread the yard treasures out on a newspaper you have laid out on a table.

Now cut a section out of the brown paper bag, and place the paper over a leaf or twig. Use the side of a crayon to rub back and forth over the brown paper that is covering the leaf. Notice that an image of the leaf will appear on the brown paper.

Use rubbings of twigs and unusual-shaped leaves, petals, and even grasses and weeds for an interesting fall picture. Be sure to try out different colors of crayons as well as overlapping some of your leaves. The finished product can be enjoyed as a picture, or you can even turn it into a note card by cutting it down to size, folding it in half, and writing a message.

274. SPUD DUDS

 The plan: Turn a potato into a well-dressed spud!

What it takes:
- Colored marking pens
- Potatoes (the number depends on how many characters you want to make)
- Colored construction paper
- Scissors
- White glue, tape
- Odds and ends, such as fabric, lace, ribbon scraps, macaroni, pipe cleaners, buttons, yarn
- Glass of water large enough to hold your potato
- Toothpicks (optional)

Use colored marking pens to outline faces and body shapes on the potato. Cut colored construction paper into arms, legs, antennae, whiskers, or tails. Glue them onto the potato. You can also dress up your potato person/animal with all sorts of odds and ends, like fabric scraps, ribbons, macaroni, and anything else you can glue on.

Need an idea? How about a *Bat Potato*? Make a mask and cape out of black construction paper. Or the *Energizer Spud Bunny* with ears cut out of pink paper, a cute bunny face, and the perfect tail out of a cotton ball. Tape an old battery to the back!

After you've displayed your potato creation, how about watching your spud sprout? All you have to do is place the potato in a glass of water so that the bottom of the potato is in the water. If your glass is so large that the potato falls to the bottom, place four toothpicks around the sides of the potato. This will support it on the rim of the glass. You should see your Spud Dud sprout in about four or five days!

275. NOW YOU SEE IT—
NOW YOU DON'T

 The plan: Water and a bit of imagination will turn your sidewalk into a picture gallery!

What it takes:

- A bucket
- Water
- An assortment of "painting tools" such as house paintbrushes, old toothbrushes, clean paint rollers, squirt bottles, spray bottles, water toys, or sponges

Splash, slosh, squirt, and squeegee. A new water sport? No, but that's what you'll hear when you start painting pictures all over your front sidewalk, driveway, or patio with "water paint," which really isn't paint at all but just plain old water. The good news is that you can make all the mistakes you want because the water will slowly disappear without a trace of its ever having been there.

All you have to do is fill your bucket with water, dip in your brushes, rollers, and sponges, fill your spray bottles or water toys, and use any outdoor surface as your canvas. What can you paint? Anything you'd like. How about creating an alligator on the sidewalk? Using your squirt bottle or water toy, draw the outline of the animal. Try using a sponge to fill in the armored skin, then use a pointy brush to draw in those sharp teeth. Snap!

If you make your alligator's snout too thin, you can always turn it into a crocodile. American alligators have broader snouts than crocodiles do. Some really big gators can be up to twenty feet long. Do you have room on your sidewalk for an alligator that big?

Think of all the other cool things you can create and paint. If you're not feeling creative you might want to "paint" your bicycle. It may need a good washing anyway!

276. HOOKED?

 The plan: Fish with a yardstick pole and a paper clip hook!
What it takes:

- String
- Yardstick
- Scissors
- Paper clip
- Plain white paper
- Pencil
- Colored marking pens or crayons
- Hole punch

Measure and cut a piece of string about forty-five inches long. Tie one end of the string tightly onto a yardstick. On the other end of the string tie a paper clip that has been halfway unfolded. It will look like a hook. Now you have a fishing pole all set for the stream.

Fold a piece of paper in half. Take your pencil and draw a large fish with the folded edge of the paper as the top of the fish. Now cut the fish out, but *do not* cut along the fold. Unfold the fish and lay it flat. Color both top and bottom of the fish with the marking pens or crayons. Then fold the paper again and with the hole punch *make a hole* through *both* thicknesses near the fish's mouth. Make several more fish, as many as you think you can catch with your fishing pole and hook.

Stand all your fish up on the floor. They will easily stand by putting the folded part at the top and spreading the two fish sections a little at the bottom.

Grab your pole and try to catch each standing fish by hooking it in the punched hole. It is a very tricky task. It's just about as hard as catching a real fish in a real stream of water!

277. A REAL ROCKER

The plan: Make a paperweight out of a rock to hold down papers and pages!
What it takes:

- An interesting-looking rock
- Old newspaper
- Paper towel

- Felt scraps, sequins, beads, and other decorations
- Scissors
- White glue
- Paintbrush
- Bowl
- Black permanent marking pen

Go outside and find a smooth rock about the size of your fist when you close it. Wash it off outside. Bring it in the house, place it on an old newspaper, and dry it off with a paper towel.

Decorate your paperweight with cutout pieces of felt, sequins, beads, or other bits and pieces that you glue on. When your rock is gorgeous, pour a little glue in a bowl and add enough water to make it runny. Use your paintbrush to brush on the glue mixture over the rocks. When it's completely dry you can add details with a black permanent marking pen.

278. GO FISH

 The plan: Catch paper-clipped fish with a yardstick pole!
What it takes:
- Scissors
- Spool or long piece of string
- Yardstick
- Magnet (horseshoe shape works best)
- Pencil
- Construction paper
- Paper clips
- Chair
- Blanket

Cut off a piece of string about forty-five inches long. Tie one end of the string tightly around one end of the yardstick. Tie a magnet on the other end of the string. This is your fishing pole and fishing line.

Use a pencil to draw ten fish about five inches long on the construction paper. Cut them out. Slip three paper clips onto each fish.

Cover a chair with the blanket. Place the fish on the floor in back of the chair. Stand facing the front of the chair, and play Go Fish by casting the fishing line over the back. Practice catching the fish hiding in the stream behind the chair, and see how many you can catch!

279. BACKYARD ANIMAL RACE

 The plan: Time yourself as you walk like animals to see which traveling style finishes first.

What it takes:
- Measuring tape
- Rock
- 18" piece of string
- Piece of paper
- Pencil
- Watch that displays seconds or stopwatch if available

Flamingos hop, ducks waddle, elephants lumber along, and springboks (a South African gazelle) bounce. You might be surprised to see which animal travels the fastest when you pretend to be that animal. Here's a chance to find out.

Find a cleared area in your yard. Measure off twenty-five feet with the measuring tape. Place a rock to show the starting point, and put an eighteen-inch piece of string across the finish line.

List four different animals with a pencil on a piece of paper. Flamingo, duck, elephant, and springbok might be the first four. Go to the starting rock. Look at your watch and say, "On your mark, get set, go!" Pretend to be the first animal listed on your paper and walk like that animal. Look at your watch as you cross the finish line. Record how many seconds it took under the animal name. Repeat for the other animals on your list.

Which animal was the winner of the Backyard Animal Race?

SIXTY-MINUTE ACTIVITIES

"I've already seen this rerun five times," or "I have a whole hour before baseball practice," or "No one can play with me!" Sound familiar? You've got **Sixty Minutes** to turn those dirty old white sneakers into *walking works of art*! You can very well have the jazziest shoes on the block, and who knows, you may start a neighborhood fad! Look ahead for other exciting **Sixty-Minute Solo Activities.**

280. WALKING WORKS OF ART

 The plan: Turn those old tennis shoes into "walking works of art"!

What it takes:
- Old newspapers
- Pair of old used-to-be-white tennis shoes
- Permanent felt marking pens

Those old tennis shoes that have seen their day can be turned into walking works of art. First, check with an adult to make sure it's okay to use them. Place your shoes on newspaper spread out on a table, and then you simply decorate those two "oldies" with designs or pictures using permanent marking pens. Multicolored checks and squares will be eye-catching, and so will "scenic" shoe pictures of palm trees and sailboats. Think up some wonderful designs and pictures. Make them simple, bold, and colorful, and they may just end up being your all-time favorites!

281. EDITOR-IN-CHIEF

 The plan: Use old newspaper headlines to send a message to a friend or family member!

What it takes:
- Old newspapers
- Scissors
- Pencil
- Plain white paper
- White glue

Look for those big headlines on the front page of an old news-paper, and start clipping away. The rest of the sections will have head-lines of different sizes, and you can clip those out too. When you have your headline clippings spread out on a tabletop, decide what message you're going to write to someone. Write it out on a piece of paper first.

To make your special message, you may use some of the words as they are, and you may need to cut up some of the other words and use their letters to make new words. Now glue your message to a blank piece of paper, being careful to line up the words and letters. Will you mail your message to a friend, or are you trying to think of a clever place to leave it as a surprise for someone in the family? Either way, you're doing a great job of editing!

282. GET TO THE POINT!

 The plan: No lines in this drawing, but you can make tiny points in a Pointillistic picture!

What it takes:
- White drawing paper
- Pencil
- Colored marking pens or crayons

Lightly sketch in a picture or design on the drawing paper with a pencil. Now put the pencil down, and from now on you're going to use only your crayons or markers. You can't draw any lines. You can only make points! Make tiny dots to *draw* your picture. Go over all of the lines you've sketched, and instead of using a crayon to draw lines, make tiny dots very close together.

If you want something to look purple, put tiny dots of blue and red next to each other. When you stand back and take a look, it will appear to be purple. Try combining blue with yellow dots. What do you get? Red and yellow dots next to each other will make the object look orange. You can make any kind of a picture using Pointillism. Can you see why this form of art is called *Pointillism*?

283. FRACTURED FAIRY TALES

 The plan: Change your favorite fairy tale until you have a brand-new story!

What it takes:
- Lined notebook paper
- Pencil or pen

Now you can rewrite a favorite fairy tale on your own. Have you ever wondered what would have happened if Cinderella's beautiful ball gown suddenly turned back into her tattered, ash-covered old clothes while she was dancing with the prince at the ball? Horrors! To make matters even worse, when she ran out of the palace hoping to hop back into the coach, she would have been stunned to find a big fat pumpkin sitting on the cobblestone street! A few scampering mice were seen hurrying into the darkness.

Keep enough of the real story so that it will be recognizable, but think up unexpected, humorous events that will turn your old fairy tale into a brand-new story that will be worth sharing.

284. A NO-CLOTHES HANGER

 The plan: Use a wire coat hanger to make a picture theme mobile!

What it takes:
- Old magazines or catalogs
- Scissors
- Poster board
- White glue
- Hole punch
- String, yarn, or ribbon
- Wire coat hanger
- Colored marking pens or crayons

Decide on a theme for your mobile, which is actually hanging art! Will it be birds, babies, or animals? How about basketball players, balls used in sports, flowers, or maybe a combination of many themes? Cut pictures out of magazines and glue them to a piece of poster

SUPER FUN FOR ONE

board. After all your pictures are glued on and dry, cut them out with your scissors. Punch a hole in the top of each picture, thread a piece of string through it, and tie it with a knot. Decide how far down from the coat hanger you want your mobile pieces to be (some will be higher, some lower), and tie the other end of the string to the straight piece of the wire coat hanger.

You can add some fancy touches to your mobile by decorating the plain side of your pictures with marking pens or crayons, keeping the same theme as the picture on the other side. Then again, you may want to write something on the blank side like a person's name or the name of the bird or animal, or even one letter on each piece that spells a word when you read the letters in order. Now all you have to do is find just the right spot to hang your work of art!

285. DATE-A-PICTURE

 The plan: Design your own calendar of upcoming events with pictures!

What it takes:
- Current calendar (just to look at)
- Plain white paper
- Pencil
- Ruler
- Black fine-tip marking pen
- Colored marking pens or crayons

Find today's date on your calendar. If the month is nearly over, flip the page to the next month. On a piece of paper make a calendar grid (the boxes on the calendar) seven columns across and five rows down. Leave space at the top of the page to write the month and year. Leave space above each column, and write each day of the week with the black marking pen. It should look just like the calendar you are looking at. Check your calendar to see where the first day starts. Take your black marking pen and number each day. Make the numbers small in the upper right corner of each box.

Now think carefully. Are there any holidays? Check the real calendar to see. Draw an appropriate picture in the holiday square: Santa Claus for Christmas, a menorah for Hanukkah, Easter basket for Easter, and firecrackers for the Fourth of July. Make your drawings colorful by using the colored marking pens or crayons.

Are there family or friends' birthdays during the month? Draw a colorful birthday cake for those special days and write the birthday person's name. Are there any other important days coming up during the month? Vacations? Parties? School holidays? Appointments? Color pictures on those days to remind you. When your calendar is finished, hang it in your room!

286. STRING BALLOONS

 The plan: Cover a blown-up balloon with string soaked in glue and it will stand alone!

What it takes:
- Balloon
- Old newspaper
- White glue
- Shallow pan
- Water
- Scissors
- Different colors of yarn, embroidery thread, or string
- Aluminum foil

Before you start, have an adult blow up a balloon and tie off the end. Then spread some old newspaper to cover your work area. Pour some white glue into a shallow pan, and add an equal amount of water. Cut lengths of yarn, thread, or string, and dip them one at a time into the glue mixture. Place the strings on the balloon by draping them over and around. Make sure that both ends are stuck down to the balloon. Keep crisscrossing the strings around the balloon until it is pretty well covered with string or yarn. There will be lots of spaces in between.

Place the string balloon on a piece of foil to dry overnight. The next day, pop the balloon with something sharp, and carefully pull the popped balloon out through an open space between the strings. You can hang the string balloons with a piece of string or fishing line as ornaments, or as decorations anywhere in your house. Try making more of these using different-sized balloons and different colors of string or yarn.

287. FOGGY ART

The plan: Layer cut-out shapes with waxed paper to create a foggy picture!

What it takes:
- Pencil
- Scissors
- White glue
- Gray, brown, and black construction paper
- Waxed paper

The gray construction paper is the background for this foggy art picture. Take your pencil and draw a long line of hills or mountains on the brown construction paper. Cut these hills out with the scissors, and glue them to the gray background paper. Tear off *two* pieces of waxed paper the same size as the gray construction paper. Glue one piece of waxed paper on top of the picture by placing a thin line of glue along the edges of the gray paper and gently pressing down along all the sides.

Cut out two or more black trees from the construction paper, and glue them on top of the waxed paper. Glue another piece of waxed paper to the picture repeating what you did before. Cut out one more large tree from the black paper, and glue it on top. Your work is finished when the glue is dry, and you notice how foggy it looks.

288. PAST/PRESENT/FUTURE

The plan: Make a "picture" portfolio of your life!

What it takes:
- Large sheet of white drawing paper
- Pencil
- Colored marking pens or crayons

Pictures can tell a story just like words, and this picture story will be all about you! First, divide a large piece of drawing paper into three equal sections with the lines going across the paper. At the top of the first section write "Past." Across the top of the middle section write "Present," and at the top of the third section write "Future."

Next, draw yourself as a baby in the "Past" section along with many of the things that tell about your younger life. You could draw some of the toys you played with, or a picture of your house. Maybe you'd like to draw a picture of your family.

In the "Present" section, draw things that show what you are doing now. How could you show that you're a student? A desk, or maybe a set of books would show that you go to school. Do you play any sports? Think about drawing a soccer ball, or maybe you play the piano or the violin. You could draw those instruments.

In the "Future" section, think about all of the things you'd like to be. A TV anchorperson, a landscaper, a dentist, a teacher, a firefighter? You can draw yourself as anyone you'd like to become!

289. FIRST AND LAST

 The plan: Make the last letter of a word the beginning of the next, all on a squiggly line!

What it takes:
• Pencil
• Piece of paper

Draw a meandering, curving line on your paper. The line should not cross itself. Make your line with wide, big curves, and connect the end of your line to the beginning where you started. Pick a spot anywhere on the line and write a word.

The next word you write will follow the word you have just written, *but* the second word must *begin* with the letter that was the *last* letter of the *first* word. Confusing? It won't be when you get going.

For example, if the first word you write on the line is LEOPAR**D**, then the next word you write must begin with the letter *D*. Let's pretend that the next word you write is DINOSAU**R**. Do you know what letter the next word on the line would begin with? You're absolutely right if you said *R*, because DINOSAU**R** ends in a the letter *R*.

Do you know what letter of the alphabet will be the very last word you'll write? Clue: Remember that the last word you write on the line will have to *end* with the same letter as the beginning of the first word you wrote. **L**EOPARD was the first word you wrote, so your last word will have to end with the letter *L*. This will be much easier to see once you start writing words on your line!

290. HALF AND HALF

 The plan: Complete the other half of a picture so you'll know the rest of the story!

What it takes:
- Old magazines
- Scissors
- White drawing paper
- Colored marking pens or crayons
- Pencil
- Ruler
- White glue

Find a picture in a magazine that you really like. It could be something scenic, or maybe it's an advertisement for something yummy to eat. The picture of a person's face or an animal also make good "Half and Half" drawings.

After you've selected a magazine picture, use the scissors to cut it out. Place the ruler on the picture, and use a pencil to draw a line that divides the picture in half. Follow the line, and cut the picture in half. Glue the half picture on the left side of a piece of paper.

Now all you have to do is finish the right side of the picture! Use your pencil to lightly sketch in the other half, and then use your marking pens or crayons to add the color. Does *your* side look like the original on the left?

291. PAPER CHAINS

 The plan: Hook paper rings together to make the longest paper chain ever!

What it takes:
- Ruler
- Pencil
- Several pieces of different colors of construction paper
- Scissors
- White glue

Paper chains go back to the days of the pioneers, and they're just as easy to make today as they were way back then. Use your ruler to measure a piece of construction paper eight inches long by two inches wide. Mark it with your pencil and cut it out. Now use this piece as a pattern to make as many additional pieces as you'd like. The more you make, the more links you'll have in your chain.

Glue one end of a strip to the other end, making a ring. Overlap the end of the strip of paper about one-half inch. Link a new strip of your paper to the first ring by putting the strip through the ring and gluing the ends together just like you did the first one. Keep adding links to your chain until you get as many as you'd like. Are you going to do every other one a different color, or are you going to make your links all the same color?

Now that you know how to make a paper linking chain, you can make smaller rings or larger rings. You can make an old-fashioned addition to any Christmas tree, or string the chains around the house for any special day!

292. CRAZY CARTOONS

 The plan: Change cartoon captions to say what *you* want!

What it takes:
- Comic section of the newspaper
- Scissors
- White paper
- White glue
- Pencil
- Black fine-tip marking pen

Is Calvin and Hobbes, Peanuts, or Garfield your favorite comic strip? Pick any comic strip and cut out the whole strip. Now you get to make up your own little story. Give the characters new words to say. This may change the whole meaning of the cartoon. All you have to do is cover up the words the characters say by using the scissors to cut a shape out of white paper that will fit nicely over the words you're covering up.

Next, glue the white paper shapes over the old words. While

you wait about ten minutes for the glue to dry you can begin working on another comic strip. When the glued paper is dry, use a pencil to lightly print the new words that the character will say. When you've got it just right, go over the pencil words with a black fine-tip marking pen or a ballpoint pen. How did you do? You just may be on your way to a cartooning career!

293. A TRUE STAND-OUT

 The plan: Make a picture that's dimensional because the subjects are "outstanding"!

What it takes:
- Pieces of construction paper of different colors
- Pencil
- Scissors
- White glue
- Colored marking pens or crayons

Select a piece of construction paper for your background piece. Decide what to draw for your picture, and decide what subjects you'll want to stand out from the paper so they'll look three-dimensional or "almost real." For instance, if you're going to draw a picture of a house with trees and flowers, maybe you'll want the chimney and the tops of two tall trees to stand out from the rest of the things in your picture. Using a pencil, draw all of the stand-outs on a separate piece of construction paper. Make small tabs that stick out on the sides of each object, just like the tabs you see on paper dolls. Cut out your stand-out pieces with the tabs.

With a pencil, draw the part of your picture that will remain flat, and color everything in. Now add the stand-out parts by folding back the tabs on the sides and gluing them to the picture, making the object curve away from the paper.

This takes a little practice, but you'll catch on in no time. If you did trees, the trunks of the trees would be colored in on the paper, and the tops of the trees would stand out because they're made from separate paper and glued on in a curving manner. What a stand-out of a picture you're about to make!

294. BE MY VALENTINE

 The plan: Make a classy, creative box to hold Valentines from family and friends!

What it takes:
- A shoe box or other box with a lid
- Red, pink, and white construction paper
- Pencil
- Scissors
- White glue
- Valentine stickers
- Paper doilies

Keep those special Valentines for years to come in a nifty box that you decorate yourself. Place one side of a shoe box on a piece of construction paper. Trace around it with your pencil and then cut it out. Do the same for all sides of the box, including the bottom. Next, cover the box with the construction paper pieces by gluing them to each side and the bottom. You may want your box to be all one color, or maybe you'd like different colors on some of the sides. You decide.

To cover the lid all you have to do is place the lid on a piece of construction paper and trace around it with your pencil, allowing about two inches extra on all four sides. Cut out the paper cover. Spread glue over the top and sides of the lid and place the paper on top. Fold the extra paper over the sides and glue it in place on the inside of the lid.

Decorate your box by cutting out hearts, letters (Be Mine, I Love You), or even your own name and gluing them on. Use paper doilies as a background for some of your cutouts, and if you have any Valentine stickers, you can really turn this into a Valentine box that may be prettier than the Valentines you'll put in it!

295. CHOCO-JUICE BALLS

 The plan: Make a gray day a glad day by mixing up these chocolate ball–shaped cookies!

What it takes:
- Plastic container with lid
- Waxed paper
- 1½ cups finely crushed chocolate graham crackers (about 10 double crackers)
- Plastic bag with no holes
- Rolling pin
- Measuring cups
- Measuring spoons
- Mixing bowl
- ¼ cup very soft margarine
- ½ cup granulated sugar
- ¼ chopped nuts (if you like them)
- 2 tablespoons orange juice
- Fork for stirring
- Chocolate sprinkles in a small bowl

Wash your hands thoroughly with soap and water. Now collect all of *What it takes*. Prepare the plastic container by lining it with a piece of waxed paper. Set this aside.

Place the graham crackers in the plastic bag and crush them by rolling a rolling pin over the bag until they are very fine. Keep the crumbs toward the bottom of the bag so they won't spill out.

In the mixing bowl combine the cracker crumbs, margarine, sugar, nuts (if you like them), and the orange juice. Mix thoroughly with a fork. If the dough does not hold together, you may have to add a little more orange juice. With clean hands, shape the dough into small balls. Roll each ball in the chocolate sprinkles. Put the Choco-Juice Balls in the plastic container and cover with the lid. Store the balls in the refrigerator until you are ready to surprise your family with a wonderful chocolate treat!

296. ANIMAL-PEOPLE MIX-UP

 The plan: Turn magazine pictures into the most hilarious animal people you can imagine!

What it takes:
- Several old magazines
- Scissors
- White glue
- Any color construction paper or poster board

The best part about this activity is that you can cut out the pictures of just about any person or animal you can find in a magazine. Look at the advertising pages for some really great pictures.

Cut out several pictures of people and animals and spread them out on a table. The fun starts now when you cut out parts of people and mix them up with parts of animals and glue them to a piece of construction paper or poster board.

How about a person with the head of a dog glued onto the body, the legs of a cat, and wings of a bird? Or maybe you'll find a terrific picture of a horse and you'll use a person's mouth to glue over the horse's mouth, and a man's legs in trousers to glue over the horse's front legs. It would look even wackier if the two hind legs were women's legs! Have fun creating these mix-ups!

297. WHIMSICAL WIND CHIMES

 The plan: Make wind chimes that will be music to your ears!
What it takes:

- Metal measuring spoons, nails, metal washers, wooden clothespins, or any other objects that will make a noise when you hit them together
- String
- Scissors
- A sturdy twig or little tree branch about 12" long

Make all your wind chimes out of the same type of material. If you decide to use metal, you can use different metal objects, but don't use wood or other materials with it because it won't be nearly as musical. First of all, cut several pieces of string just about the same length. Twelve inches will be just about right. Tie the pieces of string onto the objects. If you're using old metal measuring spoons and there are holes in the handles, put the string through the holes and tie it.

The next step is to tie the string with the objects onto the little branch. Tie the strings close enough together so that the pieces will strike each other when they're moved. About two inches apart should do it. Try several different combinations until you get just the right sound.

Now all you have to do is tie a long piece of string about eighteen inches long near one end of the branch. Tie the other end of this string near the opposite end of the branch. Hold this string in the center and you've got your wind chimes ready to hang somewhere. A patio or deck, on the branch of a tree, a back porch, or under the eaves of your roof are all places where the wind will hit the chimes. Try out your wind chimes. Take a big, deep breath and blow!

298. YOUR OWN DAILY

 The plan: Create your own newspaper!

What it takes:
- Current newspaper
- Lined paper
- Black fine-tip marking pen
- Glue stick
- Pictures (if available)
- Colored marking pens

Quickly look through today's newspaper. Notice the newspaper's name written at the very top of the first page. Notice the date and where it is placed. Notice the headlines with the biggest, boldest words on the page. Notice that the pictures always have something to do with the article written next to them. Keep all these things in your mind because they will help you in writing your own newspaper.

At the top of the first piece of paper, write a name for your newspaper with the black marking pen. Do something like *Claudia's Chronicle, The Jackson Gazette,* or *Tyler's Times.* Use your own name or town, be creative! Write today's date.

Think about the most exciting event that happened in your life today. Make a headline (extra bold) about that exciting event. Write a *short* article about it. Remember newspaper articles are not long. They just report *Who, What, Where, When* and *Why.* Do you happen to have a picture to paste next to the article? Maybe you could draw a picture.

Write articles about other events. Make a comic strip, a sports page, a page for listing the movies you want to see. Your own newspaper is sure to be a big success!

299. SHADOW SHAPES

 The plan: Make a silhouette puppet show using a flashlight!

What it takes:

- Pencil
- Poster board or cardboard
- Scissors
- Tongue depressors or popsicle sticks
- White glue
- A light-colored twin-size bedsheet or piece of fabric
- 2 chairs
- Flashlight or lamp

Draw your favorite shape with a pencil on the poster board or cardboard, and then cut it out. Did you draw a dinosaur or a person? Draw anything you'd like, but keep it simple and large. Attach the cutout drawing to the top part of a tongue depressor or popsicle stick with white glue. The tongue depressor or popsicle stick will be the puppet handle.

While the glue is drying set up your "screen" by draping a sheet or piece of fabric over the backs of two chairs that are about three feet apart from each other with the backs facing each other. Make sure that the sheet or fabric is only one thickness and not doubled over.

Hold a flashlight in one hand behind the puppet you're holding with the other hand, so that it casts a shadow on the sheet. You can also place a lamp on a table behind the sheet "screen" with the light turned on, and hold your puppet up between the "screen" and the lamp. It works better if the lamp is higher up, behind the "screen," and off to the side. To make a shadow just keep the light behind the puppet, and the puppet shadow will show on the "screen." Practice using your puppet in front of the light, and soon you'll be able to do an entire performance for your family or friends!

300. SHEET 'N' CHALK EGGS FOR EASTER

 The plan: Decorate cardboard Easter eggs using old bedsheets and colored chalk!

What it takes:
- Old newspapers
- Lightweight cardboard
- Pencil
- Scissors
- Old bedsheet (white or pastel)
- Liquid starch
- Small bowl
- Colored chalk

Cover your work area with old newspapers. Draw and cut out six egg shapes (ovals) from lightweight cardboard. Place the six egg shapes on a piece of old sheet, and trace around them with a pencil. Make your tracing line about a half-inch larger than the egg shapes. Then cut the shapes out.

Pour some liquid starch into the small bowl. Dip the cutout pieces of sheet into the liquid starch one at a time. Cover each cardboard egg with a wet piece of sheet. Trim around the sheet with the scissors to make them even.

While your covered eggs are wet, decorate them with colored chalk. The chalk colors become very bright when they mix with the liquid starch. Let your eggs dry completely before putting them into a little basket as an Easter or spring decoration.

301. COLOR AND SCRUNCH

 The plan: To turn an ordinary brown grocery bag into a tapa cloth look-alike!

What it takes:
- Brown grocery bag
- Scissors
- Crayons

What in the world is tapa cloth? It's a kind of fabric that Pacific Islanders make by beating the bark of a tree until it can be smoothed out and painted. No need to worry. You won't need to take the bark off of a tree, but you can make your own tapa cloth. All you need to do is cut out a small section of a brown paper grocery bag and draw a design on it with your crayons. Use bold lines and bright colors. Dark colors work very well. Cover the entire paper with crayons.

Now comes the fun, because you get to crumple up what you've just colored! Be careful not to tear the paper, but keep wadding it up, scrunching it, squeezing it, and twisting it over and over. After you get it in a tight ball, unwind it, and start the process all over again. You're trying to get it as soft as you can. The crayon colors are going to get mixed up, but this is all right.

After many crumplings your "tapa" cloth should feel very soft, just like a piece of real fabric. When an adult can help, have him place the "tapa" cloth colored side down on a piece of waxed paper on an ironing board. Place another piece of waxed paper over the uncolored side of the cloth and iron. This sets the colors. Instant tapa cloth!

302. SILLY SPIDERS

 The plan: Turn egg carton cups into silly spooky spiders that will put a howl in Halloween!

What it takes:
- Empty egg carton
- Scissors
- Paper towel
- Black tempera paint
- Paintbrush
- Paper clip
- Black pipe cleaners
- Beady movable eyes (or white construction paper and black marking pen)
- White glue

Use scissors to cut three or four cups off the egg carton, and place them on a paper towel. Paint them black, inside and out, and let them dry. Holding the cup with the opening facing down, use a bent paper clip to poke eight holes (four on each side) around the bottom of the widest end of the cup. On the outside of one cup, poke a pipe cleaner through one hole and out the opposite hole on the other side. Do the same with the other three holes, and you'll end up with four "legs" on each side.

Now all you have to do is bend each leg upward in the center. Glue on movable eyes or use tiny dots of white construction paper with a black dot in the center. You can make a bunch of these silly spooky spiders to stand along a windowsill or on a table. Happy Howl-o-ween!

303. WORTH A THOUSAND WORDS

 The plan: Make a picture using the *words* of the subject instead of a line!

What it takes:
- Pencil
- Drawing paper
- Colored marking pens

Decide on a subject for your drawing. Instead of making a line drawing of your subject you're going to print or write with your pencil or colored marking pens the *word* of whatever part of the picture you're creating. For example, if you're drawing a sailboat on the ocean, this is what you would do: The bottom part of the boat would be shown by writing the word "boat" over and over to make an outline shape of a boat.

The sails of the boat would be shown by writing the word "sail" over and over in the outline shape of the sails. You are using *words* to make the outline of objects instead of pencil lines.

If there is a flag on top of the sail you would show an outline of the flag by writing the word "flag" over and over. Waves in the ocean would be drawn using the word "wave" over and over, probably in a brilliant blue-green color. A cloud in the sky would be drawn by outlining a cloud shape using the word "cloud" over and over. Be colorful, using different-colored marking pens for different words, and remember that you can be as wordy as you'd like!

304. PUZZLE-TREE ORNAMENT

 The plan: Using old puzzle pieces, make an ornament to hang on your Christmas tree!

What it takes:
- Old newspaper
- Heavy paper plate
- Pencil
- Scissors
- Cord or yarn about 8" long
- White glue
- Small puzzle pieces from an old, useless puzzle
- Small paintbrush
- Silver or gold glitter

Cover your work area with old newspapers. On the flat part of the paper plate use a pencil to draw an outline of a Christmas tree and cut it out.

Fold the cord or yarn in half, and glue the two ends about one inch from the top of the back of the tree. This is the hanger. Glue old puzzles pieces one at a time to the cutout Christmas tree until it is completely covered with puzzle pieces. It will look prettier if the pieces are layered.

Brush a little glue on the puzzle tree and sprinkle with glitter. Gently shake the tree to remove excess glitter. Let the tree dry for several hours, and you'll be amazed to see what a stunning ornament you've created!

305. BACK TO NATURE

 **The plan: Use things from your own yard to make a
landscape Mother Nature would love!**

What it takes:
- Paper sack
- Sticks, twigs, grass, leaves, pods, moss, weeds, seeds, and any other "natural" things
- Old newspaper
- White glue
- Piece of poster board or light cardboard

Search your yard and garden for interesting bits and pieces that you can use to make a true-life landscape. Place these collectibles carefully in your paper sack. Next, spread your nature treasures out on a piece of old newspaper on a table, and take inventory of what you have.

Begin placing twigs and tiny leaves or parts of leaves to make a tree on poster board or light cardboard. You might want to use blades of grass or weeds to outline mountains, or just use the grass to be just what it is, grass. Glue everything on your piece of poster board, and create a landscape as you go. Pods can be rocks or boulders. Tiny twigs can be a split-rail fence. White petals from roses or other white flowers can be clouds. Lots of seeds glued close together can be a pathway in the woods. You'll come up with even better ideas. This is truly a "natural" landscape!

306. STRICTLY PRIVATE

 **The plan: Take a shoe box and turn it into a grand box
for stashing your treasures!**

What it takes:
- Scissors
- Old magazines
- White glue
- Shoe box
- Colored construction paper

Cut out pictures from old magazines for the "theme" you'd like for your treasure box. The pictures can be all on the same subject or all different. You choose. Next, glue the pictures on a shoe box, overlapping some, until it's entirely covered. Cover the lid separately. If you'd like to add construction paper cutouts of letters (maybe your name or initials), or objects, glue them on right over the magazine pictures. When you finish you'll have a one-of-a-kind "strictly private" place to store all of your special treasures.

307. TISSUE STAINED-GLASS ORNAMENTS

 The plan: Cut out all kinds of shapes from this stiff and starchy pretend stained glass!

What it takes:
- Waxed paper
- Paintbrush
- Liquid starch
- Colored tissue paper cut into scraps of different sizes
- Scissors
- Hole punch
- Ribbon or yarn

Place a sheet of waxed paper on a table. Now brush liquid starch onto the paper with a paintbrush, and place colored tissue paper scraps on top of the starch. You can overlap the colors and cover the whole piece of waxed paper with the tissue paper. Let it dry. Now cut out different shapes such as a star, Christmas tree, bells, candles, snowmen, or even a reindeer or two. You can also make these ornaments in any shape you'd like at any time of the year.

Punch a hole in the top of your ornament, thread yarn or ribbon through the hole, and make a knot. You'll be amazed at how much your ornament looks just like stained glass, especially when you hang it in front of a light or in a window!

308. FOUR SEASONS

 The plan: View the seasons all year long in your special four-seasons window!

What it takes:
- Large sheet of white drawing paper
- Scissors
- Pencil
- Colored marking pens or crayons
- Transparent tape

You won't have to wait for the seasons to change when your own "window" shows fall, winter, spring, or summer all at the same time. Choose a window in your house that's divided into panes (sections), and cut four pieces of paper to fit four of the panes. If your windows are paneless, just fold a large piece of paper in half and then in half again so you'll have four sections.

Use a pencil to draw a seasonal scene in each of the pieces or sections of paper. Use your marking pens or crayons, or both, to color your scenes. How about drawing leaves, pumpkins, corn stalks, squirrels, and apples for fall? Winter could be a snowy window of frozen ponds, snow-topped trees, and maybe even a sledding party. Create spring with tulips and daffodils, butterflies and robins if you'd like, and make summer nothing but fun with beaches, sunshine, swimming, and biking.

Now all you need to do is attach your four seasons to the window with a tiny bit of tape, and you can glimpse them any time you'd like!

309. SIMBA AND SNOW WHITE

 The plan: Put different characters in old fairy tales for a surprise ending!

What it takes:
- Pencil or pen
- Lined notebook paper

Think of your favorite fairy tales and then mix them up! With your pencil or pen write a story on the lined paper telling what would happen if characters from one story suddenly ended up in another. What in the world would a cute little lion cub like Simba be doing walking along a pathway in the forest with the Seven Dwarfs? Or can you imagine Red Riding Hood coming upon the house of the Three Bears as she walked down a forest path on her way to her grandmother's house? What would happen if she saw that the door to the house was open and she decided to venture inside? This could be trouble.

The wolf in the Three Little Pigs may be in for quite a shock if he tried to blow down the house of the witch in Hansel and Gretel. You decide the outcome when you mix and match any two of your favorite fairy tales!

310. OATMEAL BOX SNOWMAN

 The plan: Make an ornamental snowman using a bedsheet-covered oatmeal box!

What it takes:
- White cloth 24" long x 16" wide
- Round oatmeal box
- White glue
- Scissors
- 2 pieces of white thread 16" long
- Black construction paper
- Pencil
- Transparent tape
- 12" long x 1" wide strip of colorful cloth
- 2 popsicle sticks
- Brown and yellow construction paper

Cover an oatmeal box with a piece of white cloth. Pull the cloth as tight as you can, and then glue the loose edges of cloth tightly to the box. Tie the sixteen-inch pieces of thread around places where you think the neck and waist should be. Cut out eyes, nose, mouth, and buttons from the black construction paper. Glue them on the covered oatmeal box.

To make a hat, cut a three-inch-wide black paper strip long enough to go around the snowman's head, plus one inch. Glue this in place on the snowman's head. On the black paper, trace around the top of the hat to make a top for the hat. Now measure out from that circle about two inches and draw another circle. The inner circle is the top of the hat. The outer circle is the hat brim. Cut out these two circles.

Slip the brim over the hat and glue it in place. Use the transparent tape to stick the top of the hat in place. Tie the colorful strip of cloth around the neck for a scarf. Glue and tape two popsicle sticks in place for arms. Make a broom from brown and yellow construction paper. Glue it to one of the popsicle stick arms. January is a good month to display your snowman.

311. GO FOR THE GOLD!

The plan: Try your hand at designing Olympic trading cards!

What it takes:
- Ruler
- Pencil
- Poster board or tagboard
- Scissors
- Colored marking pens or crayons
- Black fine-tip marking pen
- Clear contact paper (optional)

The Olympics are now held every two years, alternating between the Winter Games and the Summer Games. Design your own Olympic trading cards showing some of your favorite Olympic events.

First, take a ruler and use a pencil to measure 2½" x 3½" on the poster board to make a card. Cut it out, and then trace around this shape for the rest of your cards. Start with four cards. You can always keep adding to your collection.

Now it's time to decide which sports you're going to feature. Keep the Summer and Winter Games separate. A few summer events would be swimming, track and field, gymnastics, and equestrian (horseback riding and jumping). The Winter Games include events such as bobsledding, figure and speed skating, skiing, and ski jumping.

Use your pencil to lightly draw your picture and the lettering which should include the name of the event and the year of the Olympics. Use marking pens or crayons to bring your new collector's cards to life! To keep your cards in tip-top shape, cover them with clear contact paper.

312. NO-COOK PEANUT BUTTER SQUARES

 The plan: Create a mouth-pleasing peanut butter bar covered with chocolate chips!

What it takes:
- 9" x 9" baking pan
- Nonstick cooking spray
- 2 cups graham cracker crumbs (about 20 double crackers)
- Plastic bag with no holes
- Rolling pin
- Large mixing bowl
- 1½ cups powdered sugar
- 1 cup chunky peanut butter
- ½ cup very soft margarine
- Fork for stirring
- 1½ cups milk chocolate chips

Get out all the things listed under *What it takes.* Wash your hands with soap and water. Spray the baking pan with nonstick cooking spray, and set it aside.

Put a few crackers into the plastic bag and crush them by rolling them with the rolling pin. Do this until all the crackers are finely crushed.

In the large mixing bowl combine the crumbs, powdered sugar, peanut butter, and soft margarine. Stir with the fork until mixed well. This dough will be very stiff.

Press the dough into the 9" x 9" baking pan. Sprinkle chocolate chips over the dough and then press the chocolate chips down into the dough with your hands. Cut into squares. When you serve these No-Cook Peanut Butter Squares for dessert, everyone will be delighted!

313. PICK YOUR OWN STORY

 The plan: The luck of the draw will guide you in writing a true original!

What it takes:
- 10 3"x 5" index cards or several pieces of plain paper
- Scissors
- Pencil
- Lined notebook paper
- 4 empty containers

Cut the index cards in half to make twenty pieces, or if you're using plain paper, cut twenty pieces of plain paper. On five of the pieces write the names of five different characters, one name on each piece. The names could be family members or friends. You can even write your own name. On another five pieces of paper write five different locations, one to a piece, where a story might take place. A cave, the ocean, the desert, ski resort in the Alps, or Disneyland, would all be interesting choices, but why not make up your own?

Take five more cards and write descriptions or time of the day or night. Examples may be descriptions like: very windy, rainy morning; the pitch black of night; late afternoon when the sun was low in the sky; crack of dawn when only the roosters are awake; or city lights were just beginning to show in the evening fog. What are some other time descriptions you could do?

On your last five pieces of paper write what kind of a story it could be. It could be science fiction, a mystery, an adventure, a comedy, or a fairy tale. You can probably think up many more.

Now all you have to do is take each group and place them in separate containers. Draw one piece from each container and see what luck you've had. The challenge is to write a story using all four story hints!

314. MAGAZINE MAGIC BEADS

 The plan: Be a jewelry designer when you make great fake tube beads out of magazines!

What it takes:
- Colorful pages from old magazines
- Scissors
- Pencil
- White glue
- String, yarn, or dental floss

Cut a triangle shape about one inch across at the base and two inches tall from one of the colorful pages of an old magazine. Use this for a pattern, and then cut about twenty of these triangles using any colorful magazine pages you like. For smaller beads, make your triangle smaller across the base and not as tall. You may even want to make bigger beads by making bigger triangles. The longer the base of the triangle, the fatter the bead.

Next, take your pencil and roll a magazine triangle over the pencil starting at the wide end and rolling toward the point at the top. Put some dots of glue in the center as you roll the paper over each turn of the pencil. Keep rolling and add some dots of glue as you roll. When you get to the point of the triangle, glue it down under the pointed end. Slide the tube bead off the pencil. Hold it in your hand until the glue sets, and then start on your next one. Make a bunch of beads, and when you're finished, you can string them together with your yarn, dental floss, or string to make a necklace or a bracelet. Tie the ends together for the finished product.

315. PET PLACE MATS

 The plan: Make a place mat for your pet so there's no more food on the floor!

What it takes:
- 18" x 24" white or light-colored construction paper
- Pencil
- Old magazines
- Scissors
- Photos of your pet
- White glue
- Colored marking pens or crayons
- Clear contact paper

No more messy floors when Max or Tiger have dinner and most of it ends up outside of the doggy or kitty dish. Treat your pet to a place mat! Take a piece of construction paper and with your pencil draw some favorite pet fantasies that your pet might enjoy. What cat wouldn't love to see a place mat covered with colorful fish? And what dog wouldn't love eating his dinner on a place mat decorated with cats?

If you really want to get fancy, find animal pictures in old magazines that you can cut out and glue onto the mat. You could also glue on actual photos of your pet and then decorate around them with your marking pens or crayons. When you're all finished with the artwork, you may need a little help to cover both sides of the place mat with clear contact paper. This way, any spills on the mat can be easily wiped off, the place mat stays perfect, and so does the floor!

316. WRAP IT UP!

 The plan: Turn a bottle into a decorated flower vase by wrapping it in yarn or string!

What it takes:
- Bottle or jar
- Yarn or string
- White glue
- Water
- Paintbrush
- Bowl
- Tempera paint

Squeeze some glue onto the top part of the outside of a bottle. Now wrap the bottle around and around with yarn or string so that it sticks to the glue. Work on small sections at a time so the glue won't run down the bottle. Don't leave any space between the rows of yarn. Next, pour some more glue into a bowl and dilute it with a little water. When the bottle is completely covered with yarn, paint over it with the diluted glue. When this is dry you can leave it just like it is, or you can paint it and decorate it with tempera paint. Either way, you'll have yourself a clever little container that can hold anything from pencils to a bouquet of flowers.

317. SHAPE UP!

 The plan: Construct crazy sculptures out of toothpicks that will look like modern art!

What it takes:
- Paper plates, dishes, or bowls
- White glue
- Flat toothpicks
- Spray paint (optional)

Use a paper plate, bowl, or dish for the base of your sculpture. Squirt a little white glue about the size of a quarter onto another plate or bowl. Dip a toothpick into the glue and place it lying down on the paper plate. Now do the same with several more toothpicks until you have an outline of toothpicks as a base, glued to the paper plate. To start building your sculpture up, simply dip each end of a toothpick into the glue and attach it to one of the base toothpicks. You can glue the toothpicks in any direction you'd like.

You can make your toothpick stick up (you may have to hold it in place a few seconds until the glue takes hold) and the sky's the limit! Build up and out, and see what kind of an amazing sculpture you can make. When it's finished, you may want to have an adult help you spray-paint it any color you'd like.

318. CARTON WREATH

 The plan: Make a Christmas wreath from a paper plate, egg carton cups, and pinecones!

What it takes:

- Old newspapers
- 2 egg cartons
- Scissors
- Green tempera paint
- Paintbrush
- Paper plate
- White glue
- 5 small pinecones
- Wide red ribbon
- Hole punch
- String for hanging the wreath

Spread old newspapers over your work area. Cut the egg cups from the cartons and paint each one with green tempera paint. Cut the middle from the paper plate and paint the "wreath" green. Glue the painted egg cups with the bottom flat side down, onto the painted "wreath" until it is completely covered with egg cups.

Glue a few small pinecones onto the wreath. Tie a bow with wide red ribbon and glue it to the wreath. Punch a hole in the top of the wreath with a hole punch, and thread a string through the hole. Tie the ends in a knot and hang your wreath!

319. IT LOOKS LIKE GLASS!

 The plan: Make stained-glass objects out of colored white glue!

What it takes:
- Old newspapers
- Pipe cleaners
- White glue
- Bowl (one or more)
- Tempera paint, a few colors
- Spoon
- Waxed paper

Spread some old newspapers out on a table, and then decide on some simple objects that you'd like to turn into fancy pieces of stained glass. Think about a simple tulip or other flowers with scalloped edges. A butterfly would also be beautiful, and so would a bluebird or a robin.

Take a pipe cleaner and bend it into the shape you'd like. Leave one end of the pipe cleaner free to use as a handle, or you can attach another pipe cleaner to your object by wrapping it around the already shaped pipe cleaner. Just remember that your object must be closed off so that no part of it is open.

Pour about one inch of white glue into a bowl. If you want colored stained glass, add a few drops of tempera paint and stir with a spoon until it's just the right color. You may want to make three or four different colors in separate bowls. Next, dip the pipe cleaner shape into a bowl of glue, holding on to the pipe cleaner handle. Be sure to completely cover the pipe cleaner shape with the glue. Remove it from the bowl and let any leftover glue drip off. Notice how the glue makes a thin coating over the entire object. If the glue gets holes in it or pops, dip the object into the glue again. Carefully place your stained-glass objects on a piece of waxed paper until they dry. Are you ready to try doing several flowers and maybe even a butterfly?

320. MOSAIC MURAL

 The plan: Use tiny pieces of cut-up construction paper to make a tile mosaic look-alike!

What it takes:
- Pencil
- Scissors
- Different colors of construction paper
- White construction paper
- White glue
- Tweezers

Sketch a drawing on a piece of white construction paper with a pencil. Use scissors to cut out lots of different colored small and tiny squares from the construction paper. Spread some glue over one part of your picture at a time, and then place the tiny squares of colored paper on the drawing. Pretend that these are tiny squares of tile, and you're making a picture using tiles. If you're having a hard time picking up the tiny squares of paper, use a pair of tweezers to help get them set in place.

321. DON'T FLIP OUT!

 The plan: Make your own animated cartoons!

What it takes:
- Several pieces of plain white paper, Post-it pads, or small notepads
- Ruler
- Pencil
- Scissors
- Stapler
- Black fine-tip marking pen

The Lion King, Pocahontas, and *Aladdin* are all Disney animated cartoons, and now you can add your own to the list. To make your own animated cartoon, you'll need to do the following: First, use the ruler and pencil to measure a three-inch square on a piece of white paper. Cut out the square. Place that square on top of two sheets of paper. With a pencil trace around the square pattern and cut out the two pieces of paper together. Repeat this until you have at least sixteen squares cut. If you have a Post-it pad or a small notepad, use these instead of cutting out your own squares.

Now stack up the little pieces of paper and staple them at the top with two staples. You have a little book that opens up from the bottom. On the first page, draw a picture with a pencil of something simple like a face. To make your animated movies, you now must draw the same face on every single page, in the same position except that each page changes just a tiny bit. If an eye is going to blink, begin by drawing an opened eye. The next page would show the eyelid barely coming down. The third page would show the eyelid a little bit lower. On each page the eyelid gets lower until it is closed! Go over your pencil lines with a black fine-tip marking pen. When you're finished, flip the pages and see how the animation works!

322. THROUGH THE PORTHOLE

 The plan: Make a porthole and see fish anywhere in your house without using water!

What it takes:
- 2 dinner-sized paper plates
- Scissors
- Blue and other colors of construction paper
- White glue
- Pencil
- Colored marking pens
- Transparent tape
- Plastic wrap or cellophane
- Stapler
- Hole punch
- 8-inch piece of string

Take one paper plate and use your scissors to cut out the center. Take your second paper plate and cut a piece of blue construction paper to fit over the inside part of the plate. Glue it on. Next, use a pencil to draw and then cut out several colorful fish of all sizes and shapes from the colored construction paper. Use your marking pens to add gills and fins, eyes, scales, spikes, mouths, and even stripes. How about a starfish or a seahorse? Maybe you'll even want a shark! Now glue your fish onto the blue background on the paper plate. Try overlapping a fish or two to make it look like one is swimming in front of the other.

When your fish are all in place, take the paper plate with the round hole in the center and tape a piece of clear plastic wrap or cellophane on the inside so that the hole is covered. Next, place this plate on top of the one with the fish (two fronts facing) and glue the edges in place, or staple together all around the edges. Add the final touch by punching a hole in the top of your porthole, pulling the piece of string through it, and tying the ends in a knot. You may now hang your porthole in a window, on a cupboard handle, or on a doorknob. Caution: Keep all cats away!

323. ZESTY APPLE BALLS

 The plan: Concoct no-bake cookie balls that people will gobble up!

What it takes:
- Plastic container with lid
- Waxed paper
- 1 cup finely crushed vanilla wafers (about 40 wafers)
- Plastic bag with no holes
- Rolling pin
- ½ cup granulated sugar
- 2 tablespoons very soft margarine
- 2 teaspoons apple juice
- 1 teaspoon lemon juice (from concentrate)
- Mixing bowl
- Fork for stirring
- Powdered sugar in a small bowl

Wash your hands thoroughly with soap and water. Now collect all of *What it takes*. Line the plastic container with waxed paper and set it aside. Put the vanilla wafers in the bottom of the plastic bag. Crush them into crumbs by rolling over the bag with a rolling pin. After each roll, shake the wafers down to the bottom of the bag so they won't spill out.

Combine the crumbs, granulated sugar, very soft margarine, apple juice, and lemon juice in a mixing bowl. Stir with a fork until everything is well blended.

With your fingers, shape the dough into small balls about one inch across. Roll each ball in powdered sugar. Put the balls into the wax paper–lined plastic bowl. Store the Zesty Apple Balls in the refrigerator.

324. JUNKYARD JUNKIE PICTURE

 The plan: Make an antique-looking picture that's filled with junk and covered with foil!

What it takes:
- Any kind of little pieces of junk such as nails, buttons, paper clips, old play rings and jewelry, string, beads, screws, bolts, bottle caps, and anything else you'd like
- Piece of cardboard the size you'd like to picture to be
- White glue
- Water
- 2 bowls
- Paintbrush
- Aluminum foil
- Liquid soap
- Tempera paint of your favorite color

Arrange your junk treasures on a piece of cardboard and then glue them on. When the glue is dry, make a glue mixture in a bowl of two parts glue to one part water. Using a paintbrush, paint over the entire board and all the junk with the glue mixture.

Next, place a piece of aluminum foil over the top of your design, wrapping it around the back on all four sides and gluing it down. Use your fingers to carefully push and mold the foil to the shapes of the junk. You can wrinkle it and crinkle it to fit everywhere.

To make your picture look like an antique, add a few drops of liquid soap to some tempera paint in another bowl, and then brush the mixture over the foil. A true junkyard antique classic!

325. QUICKSAND AND SHARKS

 The plan: Design a treasure map that even Captain Hook would envy!

What it takes:
- Pencil
- Large piece of construction paper, butcher paper, or poster board
- Colored marking pens or crayons
- Black fine-tip marking pen

Where are you going to put the *X* that marks the spot on your treasure map? To make a treasure map that Blackbeard and Captain Hook would envy, take your pencil and paper and draw a large island that almost fills up the whole page. Did you make some wavy lines that look like harbors where the pirates might land? You could even draw a pirate ship out in the ocean flying the skull-and-crossbones flag. Are there sharks in the ocean?

How about sketching a cave or a waterfall on your island? Both of these would be great places to hide a treasure chest. Another idea: Maybe the treasure could be hoisted up into a tall palm tree or hidden under the wreckage of a boat that had washed ashore. If there are native huts on your island, it's possible that the treasure was buried under one of these, or even hidden under some large boulders and rocks at the far end of the island right near the quicksand!

Color in your map, and outline the details with the black fine-tip marking pen. Are you going to put an *X* on the spot where the treasure is buried? Maybe that will be *your* secret and everyone else will have to guess the location!

326. BE A SAND PAINTER

 The plan: Make designs on cardboard with colored sand that will never blow away!

What it takes:
- Old newspapers
- Sand (different kinds if possible)
- 5 bowls
- Powdered tempera paint
- Piece of cardboard
- Paintbrush
- White glue
- Water

Spread old newspapers on a table, and put some sand in four different bowls. Add different colors of powdered tempera paint to the sand to make it colorful. If you live where there are different colors and types of sand available, you won't have to use the powdered paint. Squeeze some glue into the fifth bowl and thin with a little water. Use a paintbrush to paint designs or pictures on the piece of cardboard with the watered-down glue.

While the glue is wet, carefully sprinkle sand over the painted areas of your picture, using some of the different-colored sand for different sections. Work with one color at a time, the lightest color first, and when the sand is pretty well set, gently tip the cardboard and let any excess sand fall off onto the paper. Then move on to another color. You may have to go over some areas a second time using the same process.

327. PUNCHIES

 The plan: Make a hole-punch picture using round paper circles!

What it takes:
- Handheld hole punch
- Different colors of construction paper
- A dish for each color of paper
- White glue
- Paper or ceramic plate
- Tweezers
- White drawing paper

Use the hole punch and start punching holes in different colors of construction paper. Keep the colored paper dots separate by punching the holes in the paper over a dish. Keep all the reds together, all the greens together, and so on, in separate dishes. When you've punched several colors, you're ready to begin your picture. Squirt a little white glue onto a paper or ceramic plate. Use the tweezers to pick up one paper dot at a time. Dip the dot into the white glue on the plate. Create a work of art as you glue the dots onto the piece of white drawing paper.

Place the dots close together to give a solid appearance, or you can use the dots to outline shapes. Maybe you'll want to outline everything in your entire picture. Maybe some things will be filled in with lots of dots or overlapped. This project takes time, but you can stop whenever you'd like, and come back to it later.

328. PICNIC TABLECLOTH

 The plan: Turn an old flat bedsheet into a tablecloth you can use for family picnics!

What it takes:
- Lots of old newspapers
- Old white flat bedsheet
- Paper
- Pencil
- Permanent marking pens

This project is done best on a hard-surface floor. Spread out old newspapers on the floor, and then spread out the sheet on top. If you'd like, you can use a pencil to sketch your design first on a piece of paper. Draw your picture or design on the sheet with a pencil, and then go over all of your lines with permanent marking pens.

This is a project that you can fold up, put away, and then take out and work on whenever you'd like. Sometimes it's a good idea to get the entire sheet drawn in before you start adding the color. You might want to think about drawing a border around all four sides or maybe printing the names of your family, friends, and pets. Use your imagination, and see what fantastic theme you can come up with for this great picnic tablecloth!

329. BOX CITY

 The plan: Use all kinds of boxes to make your own city of buildings, stores, and more!

What it takes:
- Different types and sizes of *empty* boxes: shoe boxes, milk cartons, gift boxes, stationery and note-card boxes, jewelry boxes, cookie boxes, makeup boxes, and any other box you'd like
- Colored construction paper
- Scissors
- White glue
- Black fine-tip marking pen
- Toy cars, airplanes, people, etc.

Get all of your boxes, big and little, together on a table or the floor. Next, place a box on top of a piece of construction paper, and just like wrapping a present, cut the paper to fit around the box. Glue the paper onto the box. Do this until all the boxes are covered. Use your black fine-tip marking pen to draw windows, doors, signs, addresses, and any other decorations you'd like. When you're finished, arrange the buildings to look like a little city. You could always add some toy cars around the buildings and a toy airplane or two if you've made an airport. Did you make any skyscrapers? And just what is your city going to be called? *(Your last name)* + ville?

330. PUPPETS IN THE DARK

 The plan: Use a brown paper bag and a flashlight to make these "bright" puppets!

What it takes:

- Brown paper lunch bag
- Pencil
- Black marking pens
- Scissors
- Colored cellophane
- Flashlight
- String
- Masking tape

These light-up puppets look like they glow in the dark, and you can make them as scary as you'd like! Draw a spooky face on one side of the paper bag with a pencil. Make eyes, a nose, a mouth, and even eyebrows if you're creating a person puppet.

If it's an animal puppet, maybe you'll draw a snout, a beak, beady eyes, chipmunk cheeks, or cat whiskers. Make any thin lines thick, such as whiskers, because you're going to cut them out. Next, use a black marking pen to go over your pencil lines.

Now cut out the features, such as the eyes, the openings of the nose or snout, the eyebrows, the upper lip, and the lower lip (keep them separate so they'll look like a real mouth). Cut cellophane a little larger than the mouth, eyes, and other features, and tape it to the inside of the bag behind the features.

Now all you need to do is insert a flashlight into the bag opening. Use a string or masking tape to make the bag tight around the "neck" of the puppet. Find yourself a dark closet or room, and switch on the flashlight. Wow! What a bright idea!

331. JUMP-START

 The plan: Use any of these story starters to give you a jump on writing a thriller!

What it takes:
- Lined notebook paper
- Pencil or pen

"It was a dark and stormy night" is how Snoopy sometimes begins his stories, but here are some different ones that may be just what you need to write your own thriller of a short story. Get your pencil and paper ready and try one of these:

"Shimmering light streamed through the thick trees of the jungle as we cut our way through the underbrush. A shrill scream stopped us in our path as . . ."

"While I watched through the window and saw the soft flakes floating gently against the night sky, I thought about another snowfall when . . ."

"Wading through the knee-deep water, we were only a few feet from the boat when all of a sudden . . ."

"I opened my eyes and everything looked different. I even felt different. I sat up, trying to figure out where in the world I was. It didn't take long to find out because . . ."

"The flight had been perfect. The control panel hummed just like it knew we had almost reached our destination, and as I leaned back in my seat and looked out the window at the earth below I was jolted by . . ."

Why not try to think of one on your own, or ask someone to write a story starter for you?

332. HANDPRINT WREATH

 The plan: Trace around your hand and turn lots of handprints into a holiday wreath!

What it takes:
- Pencil
- Green construction paper (different shades of green look great), about 20 sheets in all
- Scissors
- Paper plate
- White glue
- Red construction paper, about 3 sheets
- Lid of a small bottle or a coin

Use a pencil to trace around your hand up to your wrist on green construction paper. Cut out the hand tracing. Use this as a pattern, and cut out about fifty more. You can sometimes cut two or three hands out of two or three pieces of paper at a time. Next, cut out the inside part of a paper plate so that a paper plate ring is all that's left. Start gluing the handprints onto the paper plate ring with the wrist part of the hand glued on the circle's inner edge. The fingers of the handprint will extend over the paper plate edge. Overlap the next handprint about three-fourths over the one you've just glued. Keep repeating this until the entire paper plate ring is covered and it looks like an evergreen wreath.

Use the lid of a bottle or a coin to trace around and make berries out of the red construction paper. Glue these in little bunches onto the wreath. Draw a bow on the red paper and glue it to the top or the bottom of your wreath. Happy holidays!

333. SOMETHING'S NOT RIGHT

 The plan: Draw your own version of "What's wrong with this picture?"

What it takes:
- Large sheet of paper, butcher paper, or poster board
- Pencil with an eraser
- Black fine-tip marking pen

You've seen those "What's wrong with this picture?" pages in magazines and game books. Now you get to try your hand at drawing your own. It's easier than you think. First, you'll need to draw a picture with a pencil of just about anything you'd like. You can draw people, animals, cars, boats, airplanes, skateboards, houses, skyscrapers, furniture, food, classrooms, toys, and bicycles. You can draw anything, but try to make what you draw look as real as possible.

The best part is coming up. Use the eraser to erase and change something about everything you've drawn so that it's *wrong*. For example, you could put a shoe on a car where a tire should be. A baseball bat could be one leg of a table, and the chair could have just three legs! A chimney could be sticking out the side of a house instead of on top of the roof, and one wing of an airplane could be upside down! Use a black fine-tip marking pen to outline the pictures, and have fun making things wrong! Now find someone to guess, "What's wrong with this picture?"

334. HOUSE ON SWEET'S STREET

 The plan: Cover a small milk carton or box with candy to make the sweetest house ever!

What it takes:
- 1 egg white in a mixing bowl
- 1 cup confectioner's sugar
- Spoon for stirring
- Rotary beater (optional)
- ½- or 1-pint milk carton, or small box
- Spatula or spoon for spreading
- Different kinds of candy: Starbursts, gumdrops, M&M's, Lifesavers, Hot Tamales, lollipops, candy sticks, and anything else that's sweet and not plain chocolate

This is the best after-Halloween activity ever, and you'll soon know why. Before you begin, have an adult separate an egg for you. After that, you're on your own! Save the egg white in a bowl, and discard the egg yolk. Slowly add the one cup of confectioner's sugar to the egg white to make the icing, and stir the mixture with a spoon until it's smooth. Use a rotary beater if it's still lumpy. Take a small milk carton or small box, and using a spoon or spatula, spread the icing all over the carton or box until it is completely covered.

While the iced carton or box is still wet and sticky, press different pieces of candy into the icing. You can make delightful designs by grouping one kind of candy. For instance, the entire roof of your candy house might be covered in brown M&M's, while the windows might be outlined with Good & Plenty pieces. A stack of Lifesavers with icing in between would make a charming chimney. Can you see why this is a great after-Halloween project?

335. LEATHER-LOOK CONTAINER

 The plan: Turn a juice can or small box into a "leather" look-alike by using masking tape!

What it takes:
- Empty juice can or small jewelry-size gift box
- Masking tape
- Brown or black tempera paint or brown shoe polish
- Paintbrush

Cover a juice can or small box with pieces of masking tape that you tear off of the roll. Make the pieces different sizes, but keep them small. Overlap some of the pieces and angle some in different directions. Do the lid separately. When the entire box and lid or can is covered, brush on brown, black, or both colors of tempera paint or brown shoe polish. Let dry completely before handling. Your container will take on the look of real leather, and become a great little storage place for your favorite things!

336. SLOT AND STICK PUPPETS

 The plan: Make stick puppets that can be moved back and forth in a slot on the stage!

What it takes:
- Pencil
- White drawing paper
- Colored marking pens or crayons
- Construction paper
- Scissors
- White glue
- Popsicle sticks or cardboard strips about 5" in length
- Ruler
- Poster board

With a pencil draw pictures of people or animals on white construction paper. Color in the pictures with marking pens or crayons, or use cutouts of colored construction paper to make hats, hair, or other features. Use your scissors to cut out the pictures, and then glue them near the top on the flat side of a popsicle stick or cardboard strip.

To make a stage for your puppets use a ruler and a pencil to draw a straight line about two inches up from the bottom of the poster board. Leaving about two inches on each end of the line in tact, cut a slit on the pencil line with the scissors. Remember not to cut through to the ends of the poster board. This is the slot for your puppets.

Design the backdrop for your puppets on the poster board. Maybe you'll decide to create an outdoor scene, or maybe you'll want your play setting to be the inside of a house such as one of the rooms where the Three Bears lived. Draw a scene and add color.

When you're ready to do your puppet show all you have to do is slip the sticks of the puppets into the top of the slot. Use the sticks that are sticking out of the bottom of the poster board as handles, and you can move your puppets back and forth across the stage.

337. FAT FISH

 The plan: Make these fat fish out of paper and then blow them up with a straw!

What it takes:
- White butcher paper or shelf paper
- Pencil
- Colored marking pens or crayons
- Scissors
- White glue
- Drinking straw

Fold some butcher paper or shelf lining paper in half from the bottom to the top. Use your pencil to draw a picture of a fish. Make it a pretty fat fish with fins and a fanlike tail, and color it in rainbow colors with marking pens or crayons. Keep the paper folded in half, and cut out your fish so that you're cutting both pieces of paper at once. Now decorate the back of the fish to look like the front you've just done.

Glue the two pieces together by putting a line of glue all around the entire edge of the undecorated side of one fish. Leave a tiny hole where the mouth is. This is where you'll insert a straw. Next, place the undecorated side of the other fish on top and press all around so they'll stick together. Push the drinking straw inside the mouth opening and glue around it. The fish needs to be tightly glued all around to keep it air tight.

In about thirty minutes when the glue is dry, blow into the straw, and watch your fish expand. Cut off the straw so that it's even with the fish's mouth, or pull it out, and glue the opening together. Hold with your fingers until it sticks. You now have a fat fish!

338. SHOE-INS!

 The plan: Slip your feet into a funny pair of homemade shoes made out of shoe boxes!

What it takes:
- 2 empty shoes boxes with lids
- Scissors
- White glue or masking tape
- 1 pair of old shoelaces or 2 pieces of yarn about 12 inches long
- Colored marking pens
- Tempera paint
- Paintbrush

You haven't worn crazy shoes until you've had these doozies on your feet! They're a great addition to any dress-up costume, and they're a hoot to walk in. The first thing you do is to use your scissors to cut a hole in the top of both shoe box lids large enough to slip your foot in.

After you've cut both holes about the same size and you're sure you can stick your foot through the hole, you're ready for the next "step."

Squeeze a line of white glue around the entire inside edge of the shoe box lid. Place the lid back on the box and press it tightly around the top edge of the box so it will be glued tightly in place. Taping the lid on with masking tape may work better with certain boxes.

After the lid is securely fastened down, carefully poke holes with the tip of your scissors, or ask an adult to do it, to make holes for the shoelaces. Look at a pair of shoes with laces and see how the holes for the laces are placed. Make three sets of two holes, each directly across from the other. Keep them close together. Lace your old shoelaces or pieces of yarn through the holes. Decorate the box with marking pens or tempera paint and a brush. When everything is dry you're ready for a walk!

339. CREATE A CALENDAR

 The plan: Use a ready-made calendar to create a design that will be yours alone!

What it takes:
- Ready-made calendar
- White drawing paper
- Scissors
- White glue
- Pencil
- Colored marking pens or crayons

Cut pieces of white drawing paper to fit over the pictures on each page of a ready-made calendar. Glue a piece of drawing paper on each page. Then decide on a theme for your calendar, and make all of your drawings to go along with the theme. If your theme is sports, think of a sport drawing you could do for September. How about football? Swimming or diving would be a good bet for one of the summer months, and don't forget ice hockey, sledding, and ice skating for those cold months of winter. After you've sketched in a month or two of pictures, start adding some color with colored marking pens or crayons to make a colorful calendar that will be your very own design.

340. OUTDOOR-BACKYARD WORD SEARCH

 The plan: Create a word search puzzle using things found in your backyard!

What it takes:
- Lined paper
- Pencil
- Ruler

Take a look outside your house. There's lots of interesting things like bushes, flowers, cement, grass, rocks, and cars. Choose ten of the things you see and write them with a pencil along the top of the lined piece of paper. Use a ruler to make twenty vertical lines running from the top to the bottom of the lined paper. You've now made a grid.

Pick one thing you saw in your yard, and write it in the squares with one letter in each square. You can write the word up and down, across, or diagonally, but just make sure you keep all the letters right next to each other so you can read the word.

Select another object from outdoors and write it in another spot on the grid. Do this until all your words are written on the grid.

Here's the easy part. Fill in all the empty squares with letters of the alphabet. When you finish, the real words will be hidden by all the other letters.

Give this Outdoor-Backyard Word Search to a friend or family member, and see how fast he or she can find the hidden words!

SUPER FUN FOR ONE

341. NO-BAKE CHOCOLATE PEANUT BUTTER COOKIES

 The plan: Make delicious chocolate peanut butter cookies!

What it takes:
- Plastic container with a lid
- Waxed paper
- 1 cup chocolate graham cracker crumbs (10 double crackers)
- Plastic bag with no holes
- Rolling pin
- Large mixing bowl
- 1½ cups powdered sugar
- ½ cup very soft margarine
- ½ cup raisins (optional)
- ½ cup chunky peanut butter
- ½ teaspoon vanilla
- Fork
- Granulated sugar

Wash your hands and get out all of *What it takes*. Line the plastic container with waxed paper and set it aside. Make graham cracker crumbs by placing them in the bottom of a plastic bag and crushing them by rolling them with a rolling pin. Keep the crackers near the bottom of the bag so no crumbs spill out the top.

In the mixing bowl combine the crumbs, powdered sugar, soft margarine, raisins, peanut butter, and vanilla. Stir with a fork until everything is mixed very well.

Using your clean fingers, shape the dough into small balls. Flatten each ball with a fork. When the balls are flattened, sprinkle a little granulated sugar on top. Place your cookies in the waxed paper–lined container and store them in the refrigerator. Share them!

342. ZIG AND ZAG

 The plan: Create your own jigsaw puzzle!
What it takes:

- Old calendar or magazine picture
- Poster board
- White glue
- Pencil
- Scissors
- Large envelope

Select an old calendar or magazine picture. Glue the picture onto poster board. Be sure all sections of the picture are tightly glued. Let the glue completely dry for about twenty minutes.

When the glue is dry carefully and lightly draw jigsaw puzzle lines on top of the picture with a pencil. If you are an expert jigsaw puzzle worker, make the puzzle pieces fairly small. If you plan to give the puzzle to a young child when it is finished, pencil in large puzzle pieces. Carefully cut along the pencil lines.

See how quickly you can put the puzzle together. On the outside of an envelope write "Zig and Zag," and store the puzzle in a large envelope so no pieces will be lost.

343. DEFEND THE FORT

 The plan: Use cardboard boxes to build a backyard fort!
What it takes:

- 4 or more very large cardboard boxes
- Black marking pen
- Colored marking pens or crayons

Forts are great places for "make-believe" games, and so easy to build. All you need are four very big boxes (more if you can find them) and some creativity. As you build your fort, imagine defending against space invaders, deciphering messages in the secret code room, braving attacks from ferocious animals. Let's get started!

Begin by drawing doors and windows on one side of each box

with the black marking pen. On the side opposite the door, draw some solid-looking bricks. From the outside, forts look like solid walls so enemies cannot break in. Color the doors, windows, and bricks with your markers or crayons. Add some other appropriate decorations such as benches under the windows, a lookout post, crossed swords, stacked firewood, lanterns, and shutters on the outside of the windows.

Forts are usually shaped in the form of a square, so when you finish coloring, place the four boxes in a square. Be sure to put the doors toward the center of the fort. There is an empty space in the middle for you. If you have more than four boxes your fort can be much bigger. You can even make one two stories high. Wow! Go ahead and defend the fort!

344. NATURE IN A JAR

 The plan: Create a beautiful dried arrangement in a clear, upside-down jar!

What it takes:
- Plastic bag
- Collection of dried plants, flowers, leaves, seeds, bark, and twigs
- Old newspapers
- Clay or play dough (about a handful)
- Clear glass jar with screw-on lid

Get a plastic bag and take a walk through your yard. Look for pretty flowers, leaves, twigs, weeds, and anything that can be used in a pretty arrangement. Carefully place them in the plastic bag.

Spread old newspapers over your work area. Get a handful of clay or play dough. Place it in the middle of the jar lid, making certain the lid will screw back on the jar when you're done. Arrange the dried plants and other items by pressing the stems into the clay. Remember, the arrangement must not be taller than the jar.

When the arrangement is just the way you like, screw the jar carefully back onto the lid. The jar must always sit upside down so your nature arrangement will stay beautiful forever!

345. THE GRAND TOUR

 The plan: Draw a map of the United States and locate places you would like to go!

What it takes:
- United States map showing the states
- Large piece of paper
- Pencil
- Ruler
- Black fine-tip marking pen
- Red, blue, green, and other colored marking pens or crayons

Look at the map of the United States. Now draw your own map of the United States on a large piece of paper and mark in each state with a pencil. This takes some time, but you'll love the results!

On your map, locate where you live and put a ★ with the black marking pen. Now begin taking "The Grand Tour." First, visit your out-of-town relatives by using the ruler to draw a red line from your city to their city. If you have lots of cousins, aunts and uncles, or grandparents living far away from you, there will be lots of red lines on the map.

Would you like to visit Washington, D.C., to see our nation's capitol? It is located between Maryland and Virginia. Find it and rule a blue line from your home to Washington, D.C. If you would like to vacation at Disneyland in Southern California or Disney World in central Florida, make a green-ruled line to those spots. Your map should be looking very colorful. Choose your own color for making lines to other places you dream of visiting.

Make a map key in an empty corner of the paper to record where the colored lines go: Relatives = red, Washington, D.C. = blue, Disneyland/Disney World = green, and so on.

"The Grand Tour" will make a great wall hanging for your room when it's finished!

346. BURY THE PRESENT

 The plan: Make a "time box" to be hidden away for at least one year!

What it takes:
- Large shoe box
- Photographs
- School papers
- Newspaper clippings
- Scissors
- A small personal treasure
- Plain white paper
- Pencil
- Plastic wrap
- Large reclosable plastic bag or one with a tie

If someone ever goes to the Moon in a hundred years or so, they will find a special box called a "Time Capsule." It is filled with things about our country and about how we live.

It is fun to make your own "Time Capsule" right now. Find a sturdy shoe box. Look for important things about you and the time in which you live. Use photographs, school papers, and newspaper articles that tell about important things in the world today, and maybe even a small special toy or treasure that belongs to you. Select a few important items and put them in the box. Write the date on a piece of paper and tape it to each item as you put them in your "Time Capsule."

When the box is full, close the lid. Write "Time Capsule" Do not open until at least_____ (select a date at least one year away). Wrap your box completely with plastic wrap and put it in a large plastic bag that you can close tightly.

Now it's ready for hiding. You could bury it in your backyard, or just put it way up in the top of a closet. One of these years it will be fun to open and have a peek at your past.

347. ORANGE PORCUPINE BALLS

 The plan: Make delicious noncook, coconut-covered, ball-shaped cookies!

What it takes:
- Plastic container with tight-fitting lid
- Waxed paper
- 1½ cups crushed vanilla wafers (45 wafers)
- Rolling pin
- Plastic bag with no holes
- ½ cup powdered sugar
- ¼ cup finely chopped nuts (if you like nuts)
- ¼ cup very soft margarine
- 2 tablespoons frozen orange juice concentrate
- Large mixing bowl
- Fork
- Flaked coconut, about 1 cup
- Pie tin

Wash your hands with soap and water. Get out all of *What it takes*. Line the plastic container with waxed paper. Set this aside.

Place vanilla wafers into the plastic bag. With the rolling pin, roll the bag until all the wafers are finely crushed. Make sure the wafer crumbs do not spill out the bag opening.

Place crushed wafers, powdered sugar, chopped nuts, margarine, and orange juice in the mixing bowl. Stir with a fork until everything is well blended.

Sprinkle coconut onto a pie tin. With your clean fingers, shape the dough into marble-size balls. Roll the balls in coconut and place them in the prepared plastic container. Store these round cookies in the refrigerator, and when your family is ready for a treat, a treat is ready!

348. TEETERING TOTEM

 The plan: Build a terrific totem pole with four empty cans!

What it takes:
- Pencil
- Ruler
- 4 empty cans the same size
- 4 pieces (different colors) of construction paper
- Transparent tape
- Scraps of colored construction paper
- Scissors
- White glue

Indians of the Pacific Northwest made totem poles to represent their tribes. Sometimes totem sections represented families in the tribe. Each section of a totem is different. Use a pencil and ruler to measure the construction paper so it covers the sides of the cans. Use a different color of construction paper for each can.

Cut out the pieces you have marked. Squeeze a line of glue around each can, and then wrap the covers around the sides of the cans. Seal the edges of the can covers with transparent tape. Each covered can will be a section of your totem pole.

Cut out decorations for each can from scraps of construction paper. Glue them on the cans. Remember that each totem section must be different than the others. One might have wings and look like a bird. The top section might look like a scary warrior with hair sticking up. You can even use decorations that represent families in your own "tribe," such as your own family or aunts, uncles, and cousins. Be creative and make each section colorful.

When the cans are all decorated, stack the cans on top of each other. Glue the sections together and put tape around the cans where they are joined. What story does your totem tell?

349. PUZZLE WREATH

 The plan: Create a wreath made of old puzzle pieces!

What it takes:
- Old newspapers
- Heavy paper plate
- Scissors
- 6" piece of heavy cord
- Stapler
- Strong mailing tape
- Small puzzle pieces from an old, useless puzzle
- Tempera paint
- Paintbrush
- iquid detergent (optional)
- Wide gift-wrapping ribbon

Cover your work area with old newspapers. Beginning in the middle of the plate, cut away the center, leaving a wreath shape. Make a hanger for the wreath by folding the six-inch cord in half and stapling the unfolded ends to the front of the wreath about one inch from the top. Cover the staple and cord ends with tape.

Glue several layers of old puzzle pieces on the wreath until it is completely covered. Paint the wreath with tempera paint. You might consider using green as the base color and painting red apples on top. Brown, orange, and yellow are good choices if Thanksgiving is near, and pink with Valentine hearts for a February wreath. Be creative! You may need to add a few drops of liquid detergent in the tempera paint to make it stick to the puzzle pieces.

Tie a large bow of matching ribbon and glue it to the top of the wreath, just under the cord hanger. Your puzzle wreath makes a great decoration for any time of the year, and what a beautiful gift it would be for someone special!

350. "A" IS FOR APPLE

 The plan: Create an ABC book for a younger child!

What it takes:
- 26 pieces of 9" x 12" construction paper
- Pencil
- Colored marking pens or crayons
- Black fine-tip marking pen
- Old catalogs or magazines
- Scissors
- White glue
- Clear plastic page protectors
- Theme folder

It's easy and fun to make a very personal and original ABC book for a little boy or girl.

Get out twenty-six pieces of construction paper. With a pencil make a large capital letter *A* and a small *a* on the first page, a large capital *B* and a small *b* on the next page, *C* on the next and so on, until you've completed the alphabet. Color in the letters and then outline all the letters with the black marking pen.

Search through old catalogs and magazines to find pictures beginning with each letter of the alphabet. Glue the pictures you have cut out on the appropriate alphabet page. Under each picture write the word it represents with the black marking pen.

When you've finished the pages from A to Z, you can cover each page with a clear plastic page protector. This will help your ABC book last a long time. Put all twenty-six plastic-covered pages into a theme folder. Then last of all, create a title on the cover of your ABC book. Maybe you could call it *"A" Is for Apple.*

351. MY OWN ALIEN

 The plan: Create an out-of-this-world "alien" by combining pictures from magazines!

What it takes:
- Old magazines
- Old newspapers
- Scissors
- White glue
- Piece of paper

Have you ever thought of being visited by "aliens" from other worlds? Here's a chance to create your own alien. Look through old magazines or newspapers. Cut out pictures of body parts such as legs, arms, heads, bodies, hands, eyes, ears, and feet. Be clever and cut out animal body parts, too.

Now you're ready to create your own alien. Arrange the body parts you have cut on a piece of paper. When you are satisfied with how your alien looks, glue everything down.

After you've created your alien creature, how about giving "it" a name?

352. TUNE UP!

 The plan: Write your own new words for an old, familiar song!
What it takes:
- Pencil
- Lined paper

There are sweet songs, sad songs, and silly songs. Have a wild hour or more thinking up new words for old songs. Once you start humming and thinking, your mind will create all kinds of new songs.

Here's an example that goes to the tune of "Yankee Doodle."

Thank you, mother, you're so kind.
You work so hard to please me.
I like it when you make me treats,
And when you hug and squeeze me.

Mother, mother, keep it up
I'm your little dandy,
When you're shopping at the store
I hope you'll buy me candy!

Now pick up the pencil and put your own clever words on paper!

353. IT'S TREASURE TIME

 The plan: Surprise your family by making a treasure-hunt game they can all play!

What it takes:
- Pencil
- 7 pieces of paper
- 6 envelopes
- Small candy treats

It's fun solving treasure-hunt puzzles, especially when you guess the right clues. In this treasure hunt you'll know the correct answers to the clues because you make them up.

First, think of six different places in your house to hide clues. For example: under your parent's bed, in a laundry hamper, in a kitchen drawer, on the sole of an old slipper, under the living room couch, or maybe under a stack of towels in a cupboard. Of course, you'll think of many more interesting places.

Now, with a pencil let your family know where to look by writing one clue on each piece of paper. You might write the following to get someone to look under your parent's bed: "Clue #1: Go to a soft place where two people spend many hours snoozing. Just remember not to get your fingers caught in the springs. Find the clue envelope, open it, and follow where the clue leads." Do not put the first clue in an envelope because you will give it to your family when the hunt starts. Remember, each clue must lead to the location of the next clue.

Okay, you're ready to write the second clue leading your family to the laundry hamper (or wherever you choose). After it's written put it into an envelope marked "Clue #2." Hide this envelope in another spot. Continue writing clues #3, #4, #5, and #6. Hide the envelopes in the spots you have selected. At Clue #6 have a treat for the family to eat!

354. HALLOWEEN DELIGHTS

 The plan: Mix up delicious cream cheese balls covered with orange sprinkles!

What it takes:
- Soft cream cheese (6 ounces)
- Cookie sheet
- Waxed paper
- Large mixing bowl
- Measuring cup
- Measuring spoons
- 5 cups powdered sugar
- ½ teaspoon vanilla
- Spoon for mixing
- Pie tin
- Orange sprinkles

Set the cream cheese out to soften about twenty-five minutes before you begin.

Wash your hands with soap and water. Get out all of *What it takes.* Cover the cookie sheet with waxed paper and set aside. Measure five cups of powdered sugar into the mixing bowl. Measure the vanilla and add it and the softened cream cheese to the contents in the mixing bowl. Mix until well blended.

Put orange sprinkles into the pie tin. With your clean fingers make one-inch balls and roll them in the orange sprinkles. Set the balls on the prepared cookie sheet. Store in the refrigerator.

You don't have to wait until Halloween to make these yummy treats. Just change the color of the sprinkles to fit the occasion!

355. HELLO, FRIEND

 The plan: Create colorful greeting cards that send a cheery "hello" to a friend!

What it takes:
- White construction paper
- Envelopes
- Scissors
- Pencil
- Black fine-tip marking pen
- Used greeting cards
- Colorful stickers
- Colored marking pens or crayons

Want to make your friends happy? Send them individualized greeting cards, created by that world-renowned artist—you! Greeting cards usually cost lots of money, but your cards will cost hardly anything at all.

Start by folding a piece of construction paper in half. Now measure it against an envelope. Will it fit? Probably not, so with the scissors trim the construction paper to a size that will easily fit inside the envelope.

Now, think of a clever word or two that will make your friend smile, and with a pencil lightly write the words somewhere on the folded construction paper. If you write something like "Have a Great Day," you can place it either on the outside or inside of the card. Longer messages definitely belong inside the card. After your writing looks okay in pencil, use the black fine-tip marking pen to trace over the letters so they'll stand out.

Decorate the card by cutting out pretty pieces from old greeting cards. Paste on stickers if you have them. Colored marking pens or crayons can be used for drawing your own creations. When the card is decorated, put it in the envelope, and address it to a friend.

356. ANIMAL BINGO

 The plan: Make Animal Bingo cards for the family's next bingo game!

What it takes:
- White 9"x 12" construction paper
- Scissors
- Ruler
- Black fine-tip marking pen
- Colored marking pens
- 2 small paper bags
- Handful of dried beans or pennies

Fold and cut the white construction paper in half, making one half for each member of your family. On each paper half, make a grid of six rows across and five columns down. Write the letters BINGO in each one of the five spaces across the top row. Write FREE in the middle space.

Choose eight animals to draw with colored marking pens like: cat (gold), dog (brown), pig (pink), horse (red), elephant (gray), alligator (green), duck (yellow), and bird (blue). Use only one color for each animal. Draw one of these animals, or any you choose, in each square until every square (except FREE) has an animal. Make each card different, but only use the animals you've selected. Your Animal Bingo cards are ready when all the spaces except FREE are filled with animals.

When playing Animal Bingo, animal names are called instead of numbers. On a new piece of construction paper draw a grid with five columns and eight rows. Write an animal name and a letter from the word BINGO in each square. Cut out the squares. Put them in a bag ready for the caller.

Get a handful of dried beans or pennies to use as markers. Put them in another bag, and you are ready to play Animal Bingo whenever your family gets together for some fun!

357. COLLAGE ON CARDBOARD

 The plan: Collect pictures of one subject and create a collage on cardboard!

What it takes:
- Old magazines and old newspapers
- Scissors
- Cardboard (about 14" x 16")
- White glue
- Water
- Bowl
- Paintbrush

The most important thing before starting a collage is to choose a subject. You could do wild animals, golf, baseball, high fashion, funny faces, comics, or famous people. You decide. And when you've determined the subject, search through old magazines and old newspapers for pictures about the subject. Cut out as many pictures as you can find.

Arrange the pictures on top of the piece of cardboard. Is every bit of the cardboard covered by pictures? No? Then search through more magazines and newspapers until you've collected enough pictures to completely cover the cardboard. Arrange the pictures in an artistic way. They should overlap each other.

Now begin the glue job. Start at the top and carefully paste each picture onto the cardboard. Be careful not to use too much glue. When all the pictures are secured, allow the glue to dry.

When the pictures are completely dry you may want to mix equal parts glue and water in a bowl and brush the mixture on the collage with a paintbrush. This coating will dry clear and seal your collage.

358. DESIGN-A-CAR

 The plan: Build a futuristic, one-of-a-kind car of your own!

What it takes:

- Old newspapers
- Masking or transparent tape
- 2 small boxes (jewelry size)
- Aluminum foil
- Many 4" x 1" newspaper strips
- 1 cup water + 1 cup flour mixed until creamy or papier-mâché glue
- Pencil
- Poster board scraps
- Paintbrush
- Tempera paints in many colors

You might think that only boys can design cars, but some of Detroit's best automobile designers are women! Everyone can enjoy this activity. First cover your work area with old newspapers. Now tape your two small boxes together side by side to form the base for your car. Next loosely crush aluminum foil over and around the boxes until your the boxes begins to take on the shape of a car. By pushing and pressing you can make the car body any shape you want.

When your car looks just right, get out your newspaper strips and one at a time dip them into the glue mixture and start covering your car. Lightly press each wet strip to exactly fit the car shape. Add at least two layers of newspaper strips, and let the glue dry between layers.

When the glue is all dry, add car details by drawing car parts with your pencil on poster board scraps. You could draw wheels and windows. Little mirrors and headlights could be made with little pieces of aluminum foil. Cut out all your car details and glue them to your car. Now paint your one-of-a-kind car with your favorite color, and maybe someday you'll be designing for Cadillac or Lexus.

359. LIGHTS, CAMERA, ACTION

 The plan: Write your own movie script!

What it takes:
- Lined paper
- Pencil
- Short story with lots of action
- Red, blue, and green colored pencils
- Paper clip

Just pretend you are sitting in a dark theater, the screen lights up, and there in blazing color is your name as writer, producer, and director of the movie. How thrilling! Stretch your imagination and creativity, and move into the world of moviemaking.

Before any movie is made there has to be a story. If you're feeling very creative, get out paper and pencil and write your own exciting adventure tale. A faster way is to choose a *short* favorite adventure from a book you've read and use this for your plot.

Movies are made up of scenes. Think about the story you've chosen. Where does the story begin? On a piece of paper write *Scene #1* with a pencil and then write where the story takes place and what happens. Think about the story again. What happens in *Scene #2*? On a different piece of paper write about *Scene #2*. On separate pieces of paper write about *Scene #3, Scene #4,* and so on. For your first movie script, it's best not to have too many scenes.

On each scene page write in *red pencil* the *names of the characters* in that scene. Write where the scene takes place in *blue*. In *green*, write what special *equipment* is needed.

Now go back over each scene and write the words each person will say and how they should act.

Paper-clip all the scenes together and save it for a future family moviemaking time!

360. A VERY STUFFY PICTURE

 The plan: Create a stuffed fabric picture!

What it takes:

- Old newspapers
- Ruler
- 7" x 9" piece of white fabric
- Pencil
- Permanent colored markers or fabric paint
- White glue
- 10" x 12" piece of solid color fabric (not white)
- Cotton balls or pillow stuffing
- Hole punch
- 12" piece of yarn

Cover the work area with old newspapers. On the seven-by-nine-inch white fabric use a pencil to draw a picture and then color it in with the permanent markers.

On the *back* of your picture fabric squeeze a thin line of white glue on *any three* edges. Glue the picture to the ten-by-twelve-inch piece of colored fabric. There will be an edge of the dark fabric showing. Let it dry completely.

Push cotton balls or stuffing into the open end. Be careful not to stuff it too full or the glued edges will come apart. Squeeze a line of white glue under the open edge of your picture. Press firmly and let it dry.

Use the hole punch to punch two holes in the top of the larger piece of fabric, about one inch from each edge. Thread the ends of the yarn through each hole and tie a big knot in both ends of the yarn so it won't slip through when you hang it on the wall.

361. TOM TURKEY FOR YOUR TABLE

 The plan: Create a colorful construction-paper turkey with fingerprint feathers!

What it takes:
- Old newspapers
- Ruler
- Pencil
- Scissors
- 6" x 9" light orange or tan construction paper
- 3" x 9" brown construction paper
- 1½" x 6" tan construction paper
- 3 wet sponges
- 3 pie tins
- Tempera paint in brown, yellow, orange
- White glue
- Scraps of construction paper

Cover your work area with newspaper. With a ruler and pencil measure and cut the strips of construction paper listed in *What it takes*. Place the wet sponges in the three pie tins. Pour tempera paint over the sponges, one color for each sponge. These sponges are fingerprint pads. Place four fingers of one hand on one of the fingerprint pads, one color at a time, and with your fingers spread apart, press down on the six-by-nine-inch light orange paper. With your other hand, repeat this process using another paint color. The paint fingerprints are feathers. Make many fingerprint feathers using all three colors. Just remember to use one color at a time. Let it dry.

Wash and dry your hands. Now roll the three-by-nine-inch brown paper into a tube. Glue the edges down. Do the same thing to the one-and-a-half-by six-inch tan paper strip. The large tube is the turkey body. The small tube is the head. Glue the head to the body. Cut the eyes, beak, wattle, and turkey feet from construction paper scraps and glue them on. When the feathers are dry, cut them out in the shape of a fan with points up to look like feathers. Glue the feathers to the body. Gobble! Gobble!

362. CUT THE GLARE

 The plan: Make personalized sunglasses that will be the coolest shades in town!

What it takes:
- Mirror
- 12" ruler
- 9" x 12" poster board
- Pencil
- Colored marking pens
- Scissors
- Colored cellophane
- Glue stick
- White glue

Look in a mirror and measure the distance between the outside corners of each eye. This is how wide glasses should be for your face. Write the number of inches lightly on a corner of the poster board with a pencil. Measure from the side of one eye to the back of your ear and write the number lightly on the corner of your poster board. Add the total inches you need (middle + side + side = total inches needed).

Fold the poster board in half the long way. Along the fold measure and draw a line the total inches needed. Measure from the ends in and put a pencil mark where the glasses will bend for the side pieces. (You wrote the number of inches in a corner of your poster board.) Glasses are about two inches deep, so measure down two inches and draw a straight line. Make a mark in the middle of the long line. With the ruler, make a triangle ($\triangle$) from the middle mark to the line below. This is where your nose will fit. With the colored marking pens design wide frames and side pieces for your glasses. Be creative! Cut out your glasses. Do not cut along the fold. When cutting out the eye section, start in the middle and try to make both sides the same. Insert a piece of colored cellophane between the double glasses and glue it in place. Now put on those shades!

363. OVER 'N' UNDER WOVEN MAT

 The plan: Weave construction paper into a beautiful woven mat!

What it takes:
- 2 pieces of 9" x 12" contrasting colored construction paper
- Pencil
- Ruler
- Scissors
- White glue
- Clear contact paper

On one of the pieces of construction paper, use a pencil and a ruler to draw a line one inch from the edge of the paper all the way around. The ruler will help keep the line straight and even. This will be the margin.

Inside the margin measure and draw vertical (up and down) lines one inch apart going the 12" direction. Cut along each of the vertical lines. Do not cut in the margins! The cutting is easy if you lightly fold the paper in the middle and start cutting on this fold with your scissors.

On the other piece of construction paper measure and cut one-inch-wide horizontal (side to side) strips going the nine-inch direction. These are weaving strips. Start weaving by gently pushing a weaving strip *over* and *under* the vertical cuts in the first piece of paper. When the first strip is in place push it to the top of the paper and put a drop of glue on each end. Begin the next row of weaving by starting the strip *under* instead of over. Alternate each row of strips with one starting *over* and the next row starting *under*.

When you have woven as many strips as possible you have created a colorful mat. To make your mat waterproof, cover it with a piece of clear contact paper. How about placing your mat under a beautiful vase of flowers?

364. MAKE-BELIEVE STORY MAPS

 The plan: Make your favorite story come alive by creating your own story map!

What it takes:
- Large sheet of white paper
- Pencils, crayons, markers

Think of your favorite fairy tale or make-believe story. *Cinderella, Little Red Riding Hood, The Wizard of Oz, The Lion King, Beauty and the Beast,* and *Snow White and the Seven Dwarfs,* are just a few ideas. Now picture in your mind all the locations where these stories takes place. These places are called the setting. The setting changes when different things happen in the story. For instance, if you're thinking of *Snow White and the Seven Dwarfs,* you may picture the wicked queen's castle, the seven dwarfs' cottage, the mine where the dwarfs worked, the forest, the palace of the handsome prince, the houses in the little village, and maybe even some streams and mountains.

Now think of all the areas and special places you want to show on *your* map. Don't forget that you can consider including any or all of the main characters on your story map, such as the wicked queen standing in front of the magical mirror in her castle. Maybe you can show the dwarfs walking with their picks to the mine.

Once you've selected a fairy tale, begin creating your story map. Use a pencil to lightly sketch the different places and locations of the settings on the large sheet of white paper or poster board. When you have drawn everything, color your story map with markers or crayons.

Can you think of other stories that would make a wonderful map? Be colorful and creative. Maybe your setting will be more creative than the original!

365. COOL COOKIES

 The plan: Surprise everyone with this delicious treat you made all by yourself!

What it takes:

- 1 stick or ½ cup of butter or margarine, softened
- 1 11–12 oz. box of vanilla wafers
- 1 gallon-size reclosable plastic bag
- Rolling pin
- Large bowl
- 1 1-pound box of powdered sugar
- 1 6-ounce can of frozen orange juice
- Large spoon
- Rainbow or chocolate sprinkles
- Waxed paper or cookie sheet

Your family and friends will love these really **Cool** orange **Cookies**, and the best part is, you don't have to bake them! Just make sure that before you begin you wash your hands really well with soap and water.

Leave the butter or margarine out to soften for about twenty minutes. While you're waiting, place about five vanilla wafers into the plastic bag, then take a rolling pin and roll it over the bag of wafers until they are all crushed. When you've finished, pour the crushed wafers into a large bowl. Add the softened butter or margarine and the box of powdered sugar to the crushed wafers. Next, add the can of frozen orange juice and let the whole mixture rest for about ten minutes before you mix it all together with a large spoon.

Using your hands, shape a small amount of dough into a ball about the size of a golf ball. Roll some (or all) of the ball cookies in the rainbow or chocolate sprinkles. Place the balls on waxed paper on a cookie sheet. Put them into the refrigerator until they set (about one-half hour), then proudly share your scrumptious Cool Cookies with everyone!

366. A SPECIAL ACTIVITY FOR A SPECIAL DAY

This once-a-year, one-of-a-kind, one-and-only, super-duper activity is different from all the other activities in this book. It's that cake and ice cream, party, and play day. It's your birthday!

 The plan: Celebrate your birthday in a big way by making a hip-hip-hooray, razzle-dazzle, rip-roaring, razz-a-ma-tazz, sis boom ba BIRTHDAY DECLARATION!

What it takes:
- Poster board
- Pencil
- Colored marking pens or crayons

A few days before your birthday let your imagination soar to the far reaches of the galaxy. Now's your chance to pull out all the stops and put those wild, wondrous dreams into words. Make a far-out, just-for-the-fun-of-it declaration of all the outrageous things you've ever wanted to do. Put it in writing, add a splash of color (to get people's attention, of course), and then post your *Birthday Declaration* the day of your birthday on your front porch, the garage door, on the refrigerator, anywhere—for the whole world (at least your family and friends) to see.

Here's what you do: Take a good-sized piece of poster board, pick up a pencil, and print *Birthday Declaration of (your name)* in big, bold letters across the top of the poster board. You may also want to print the date of your birthday just in case someone asks.

Now comes the good part. Think of five to ten things that you'd *love* to do if you could. How about announcing to the world that on your birthday you wish to sample every ice-cream flavor ever made? Maybe you'll want to declare that you would love to spend your birthday with your number-one sports personality or TV star. What a treat that would be! What about having one-million dollars to spend in your all-time favorite store? Wow! You've got the idea, so go for it. You never know if someday your wish will come true!